Incredible
VEGAN
Ice Cream

Incredible

VEGAN

Ice Cream

Decadent, All-Natural Flavors Made with Coconut Milk

Deena Jalal

Founder of FoMu

PAGE STREET
PUBLISHING CO.

PAGE STREET
PUBLISHING CO.

First published in 2019 by
Page Street Publishing Co.
27 Congress Street, Suite 1511
Salem, MA 01970
www.pagestreetpublishing.com

Distributed by Macmillan, sales in Canada by The Canadian Manda Group.

24   23   3 4 5

ISBN-13: 978-1-62414-785-2
ISBN-10: 1-62414-785-2

Library of Congress Control Number: 2018961069

Cover and book design by Kylie Alexander for Page Street Publishing Co.

Photography by Emily Kan
Cover image © Emily Kan

Printed and bound in China

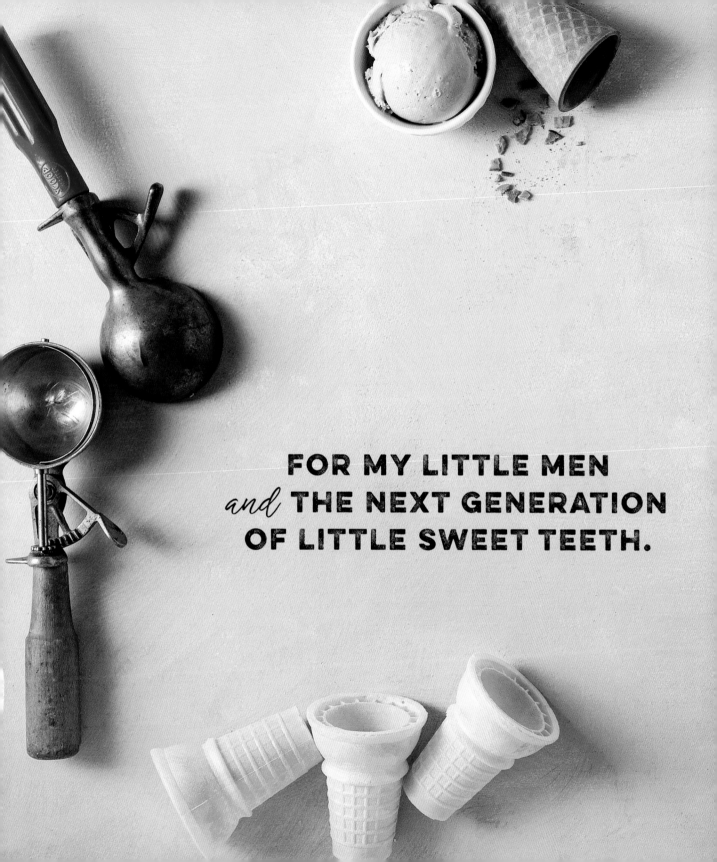

FOR MY LITTLE MEN
and THE NEXT GENERATION
OF LITTLE SWEET TEETH.

TABLE *of* CONTENTS

INTRODUCTION

When a new customer walks into one of our ice cream shops, their first question is always, "What exactly is FoMu ice cream?" To be honest, it has taken years for me to be able to sum it up in a couple of words.

"It's delicious coconut milk ice cream made with all-natural, plant-based ingredients," I'll say, "and you have to taste it to believe it." And they always do.

When you stop to think about it, the idea of vegan ice cream does seem like an oxymoron. How could a product with "cream" in the name possibly taste good with anything other than its traditional dairy namesake? Well it can, and it does, and it's easier than it seems. So why vegan ice cream?

I didn't eat much dessert growing up. My mom was a dental hygienist, and my parents bought very little prepared food. Let it be known—NO ONE wanted to trade lunch with me. Once in a while, we would have all-natural vanilla ice cream in the freezer. Always vanilla, always the same brand. Why? "It has the fewest ingredients and nothing artificial." That long-standing philosophy shaped how I eat and raise my kids today.

When I started FoMu, I wanted to make ice cream that was indulgent, but thoughtfully made. Something that satisfied your sweet tooth, but used ingredients you recognized and respected. I decided to almost exclusively use coconut milk for our signature ice cream. It is creamy, allergy friendly, and, most importantly, a deliciously simple building block to build an ice cream base. The hardest part was finding accompaniments that shared the same principle. So I made those, too. It gave me free range to dream up just about any flavor—flavors that are simple to make but that eat like a composed dessert. Over the years, we have made hundreds of flavors, from the classics to some totally wacky combinations. In the following chapters, you will find recipes for just about every season and every craving. Make the recipes as intended, or get creative. Sure you can buy ice cream, but making it from scratch is fun, simple, and out-of-this-world delicious.

There are no animal products used in any of these recipes, but taking the extra step to choose all-natural, organic, and sustainable ingredients will ensure that you are making thoughtful choices. Most importantly, always (and I mean ALWAYS) choose a full-fat, canned coconut milk. It is less processed and contains all of the natural fats needed to make a super creamy ice cream. The coconut milk "beverage" you put in your coffee is mostly water and emulsifiers and will make a terrible ice cream. Many people do taste a hint of coconut in the recipes, but the level varies quite a bit in each recipe. It is surprisingly versatile and complements just about every flavor we've dreamt up!

Once you make your ice cream, it will most likely get gobbled up immediately, but if you have more self-control than I do you can store it in an airtight container for a week or two. It won't go bad, but you may notice the flavor or texture start to deteriorate with time, especially if it is taken in and out of the freezer. It is ideally consumed at about 12°F (-11°C), which is 12 degrees higher than most household freezers. Patiently leave the pint out for 5 to 10 minutes before scooping for the ideal ice cream experience—but I won't judge if you start spooning away immediately!

Whether you are vegan, health-minded, or a straight-up ice cream connoisseur, these recipes are sure to satisfy your sweet tooth. And when people say, "but it's not REAL ice cream," be sure to point out all of the real, deliciously recognizable ingredients in what is about to become their favorite ice cream. To thoughtful indulgence. . . .

FROM *Your* CHILDHOOD

This chapter is full of recipes that will bring you back to your youth. No matter where you grew up or how often you ate ice cream, these flavors are probably the first to come to mind when you think of it. While traditional in name, they are unconventional in composition: Creamy coconut milk and smooth agave replace heavy cream and corn syrup, while whole vanilla beans, fresh strawberries, and homemade chocolate cookies turn these classic flavors into the next generation of family favorites. Every recipe is built from scratch with real, plant-based ingredients and will taste even better than you remember. You will always want to have these timeless classics in your freezer, ready to smash between two freshly baked cookies or top your favorite pie.

VANILLA BEAN

Makes 1 quart (272 g)

· ·

2½ cups (600 ml) all-natural canned coconut milk

⅓ cup (67 g) organic unrefined cane sugar

¼ cup (60 ml) organic agave

1 tsp pure vanilla extract

1 vanilla bean, with seeds scraped out

Pinch of sea salt

An ice cream–making veteran once told me that the best way to judge an ice cream brand is by its vanilla flavor. He was totally right; vanilla unveils the quality of the texture and the ingredients. This recipe uses pure and simple ingredients to reveal ice cream at its finest. Be sure to use a high-quality pure vanilla extract and real vanilla beans. I default to a 100 percent pure Madagascar Vanilla extract, but you can use Tahitian Vanilla for a super-luxurious sweet treat. Vanilla is a foundational flavor in any ice cream repertoire, whether you're serving it à la mode or sandwiched between fresh cookies.

Use a high-speed blender, immersion blender, or whisk to thoroughly mix all of the ingredients. Pour the mixture into a container, seal, and chill it for at least 1 hour, or overnight.

Add the chilled mixture to your ice cream maker and churn it according to the manufacturer's instructions. Most machines take 10 to 15 minutes depending on the temperature of the mix, and when it's finished it should look like soft serve. Once the mixture is churned, transfer it to a large freezer-safe container. Wide and shallow containers work well for mixing, freezing, and scooping later on. Smooth the top, cover the ice cream, and freeze it for at least 5 to 6 hours, or until it is firm.

Depending on the temperature of your freezer, you may want to set the ice cream out for 5 to 10 minutes to soften it before serving. This ice cream will keep in the freezer for a couple of weeks in an airtight container, but it's best when fresh.

Note: Bake up a batch of Salted Chocolate Chip Cookies (page 115) to make ice cream sandwiches. Roll the edges in chocolate chips or sprinkles for an extra special treat.

CHOCOLATE PUDDING

Makes 1 quart (272 g)

· ·

2½ oz (70 g) premium Dutch-process cocoa, weighed

2½ cups (600 ml) all-natural canned coconut milk

¼ cup (50 g) organic unrefined cane sugar

½ cup (120 ml) organic agave

Pinch of sea salt

2 tbsp (30 ml) espresso (optional)

I am going to go out on a limb and say that this is probably one of the best chocolate ice creams you will ever make or eat. It is rich and dense and reminiscent of a homemade chocolate pudding—hence the name. The ingredients are simple, so source the best quality versions you can find. I use a super high-quality Dutch-process cocoa for a smooth and rich chocolatey scoop, and I recommend using a fair trade and sustainable variety whenever possible. You can also add high-quality espresso to deepen the chocolate flavor.

Sift the cocoa and set it aside. Use a high-speed or immersion blender to mix the coconut milk, sugar, agave, salt, and the espresso, if you're using it. Add the cocoa and blend the ingredients until they are thoroughly combined. Chill the mixture for at least 1 hour, or overnight.

Add the chilled mixture to your ice cream maker and churn it according to the manufacturer's instructions. Most machines take 10 to 15 minutes depending on the temperature of the mix, and when it's finished it should have the consistency of soft serve. Transfer the ice cream to a large freezer-safe container. Wide and shallow containers work well for mixing, freezing, and scooping later on. Smooth the top, and cover it. Freeze it for at least 5 to 6 hours or until it is firm.

Depending on the temperature of your freezer you may want to set the ice cream out for 5 to 10 minutes to soften it before serving. This ice cream will keep in the freezer for a couple of weeks in an airtight container, but is best when it's fresh.

NATURAL PEANUT BUTTER

Makes 1 quart (272 g)

. . . .

2½ cups (600 ml) all-natural canned coconut milk

¼ cup (50 g) organic unrefined cane sugar

3 tbsp (45 ml) organic agave

1 tbsp (15 ml) maple syrup

12 oz (340 g) all-natural peanut butter, weighed

Pinch of sea salt

My husband eats peanut butter every day. It always makes an appearance at breakfast and usually shows up for a snack and dessert later on. When he's faced with ice cream flavor decisions, peanut butter variations always prevail. Peanut butter is obviously tasty, but it also contains protein and healthy plant-based fats. It makes for a super smooth ice cream base—just remember to buy an all-natural, non-hydrogenated, sugar-free version. The best peanut butter is exactly that: peanuts pulverized into butter. Nothing more is necessary.

Use a high-speed or immersion blender to thoroughly mix all of the ingredients. Chill the mixture in a sealed container for at least 1 hour, or overnight.

Add the chilled mixture to your ice cream maker and churn it according to the manufacturer's instructions. Most machines take 10 to 15 minutes depending on the temperature of the mix, and when the ice cream is finished, it should look like soft serve. Once it's churned, transfer the ice cream to a large freezer-safe container. Wide and shallow containers work well for mixing, freezing, and scooping later on. Smooth the top, cover the ice cream, and freeze it for at least 5 to 6 hours, or until it is firm. If the ice cream does not fully set, it will compromise the quality of the finished product.

Set your ice cream out for 5 to 10 minutes to soften it before serving for an ideal texture. This ice cream will keep in the freezer for a couple of weeks in an airtight container, but it's best when fresh.

COOKIES (& COOKIES) & CREAM

Makes 1 quart (272 g)

. . . .

2⅔ cups (640 ml) all-natural canned coconut milk

⅓ cup (67 g) organic unrefined cane sugar

3 tbsp (45 ml) organic agave

1 tsp pure vanilla extract

Pinch of sea salt

1 vanilla bean, with seeds scraped out (optional)

6 oz (140 g) Chocolate Sandwich Cookie (page 116), chopped

My oldest son, Kellan, LOVES cookies and cream ice cream. Let's be honest: the entire reason he—or anyone—loves cookies and cream is for the cookies. The ice cream is just a creamy, sweet vehicle to transport the yummy cookie chunks. So why not indulge that cookie-loving kid inside? I add tons of homemade chocolate sandwich cookies to this recipe and try to keep the chunks large. You will want to use 100 percent pure vanilla extract and vanilla beans. Tahitian Vanilla would make this one truly spectacular, but any real, good-quality vanilla will do.

Use a high-speed or immersion blender or whisk to thoroughly mix the coconut milk, sugar, agave, vanilla extract, salt, and vanilla bean, if you're using it. Chill the mixture in a sealed container for at least 1 hour, or overnight.

Add the chilled mixture to your ice cream maker and churn it according to the manufacturer's instructions. Most machines take 10 to 15 minutes depending on the temperature of the mix, and when it's finished it should look like soft serve and will hold loosely to the paddle. Once it's churned, transfer the ice cream to a large freezer-safe container and gently fold the chocolate cookie chunks into it until they're evenly distributed. Smooth the top, cover the ice cream, and freeze it for at least 5 to 6 hours or until it is firm.

Set your ice cream out for 5 to 10 minutes to soften it before serving for an ideal texture. This ice cream will keep in the freezer for a couple of weeks in an airtight container, but it's best when fresh.

SALTED CARAMEL

Makes about 1 quart
(272 g)

....

1 cup (200 g) organic unrefined cane
sugar, divided

3 cups (720 ml) all-natural canned
coconut milk, divided

Heavy pinch of sea salt

I love caramel. I always gravitate toward caramel desserts and certainly caramel ice cream. This recipe uses a dry coconut milk caramel to flavor the base. Dry caramel is made by simply melting down sugar until it liquefies, which intensifies its flavor and infuses a concentrated, rich, toasted sugar flavor with a hint of coconut. It may sound intimidating, but it actually comes together really easily. A heavy pinch of sea salt elevates the flavor and balances the sweetness. It is a staple ice cream flavor to enjoy on its own, in an affogato, or with a scoop of apple pie!

Make the caramel first. Add ¾ cup (150 g) of sugar to a medium-sized heavy saucepan over medium-high heat. Let it sit in an even layer until you see the sugar start to liquefy, about 5 minutes. If necessary, whisk briefly to dissolve larger lumps. When the sugar is completely liquefied and amber in color, slowly whisk in 1 cup (240 ml) of the coconut milk until you have a smooth, thick caramel. Remove the pan from the heat, add the salt, and let it cool.

Use a high-speed or immersion blender or whisk to thoroughly mix the remaining 2 cups (480 ml) of coconut milk, ¼ cup (50 g) of sugar, and the cooled salted caramel. Chill the mixture in a sealed container for at least 1 hour, or overnight.

Add the chilled mixture to your ice cream maker and churn it according to the manufacturer's instructions. Most machines take 10 to 15 minutes depending on the temperature of the mix, and when it's finished it should look like soft serve. Once it's churned, transfer the ice cream to a large freezer-safe container. Wide and shallow containers work well for mixing, freezing, and scooping later on. Smooth the top, cover the ice cream, and freeze it for at least 5 to 6 hours or until it is firm.

This ice cream will keep in the freezer for 1 week in an airtight container, but is best when it's fresh.

Note: Balance the smooth, sweet flavor of caramel with a crunchy and slightly savory addition of Candied Cacao (page 132).

TRIPLE CHOCOLATE BROWNIE

Makes about 1 quart
(272 g)

. . . .

1½ cups (360 ml) all-natural canned
coconut milk

2 tbsp (25 g) organic unrefined cane
sugar

⅓ cup (80 ml) organic agave

2 oz (56 g) premium Dutch-process
cocoa, weighed

Pinch of sea salt

4 oz (112 g) Double Chocolate Brownies
(page 120), cut into 1-inch (2.5-cm)
chunks

2 oz (56 g) dark chocolate chips or dark
chocolate bar, roughly chopped

Truth be told, I am not a chocolate gal. I choose spice or fruit over chocolate most days, but this recipe is an exception: Rich chocolate ice cream, chewy homemade brownie, and dark chocolate chips make this an irresistible flavor even for the declared non-chocoholic. Use a super high-quality Dutch-process cocoa and vegan dark chocolate for the best flavor and texture.

Use a high-speed or immersion blender to mix the coconut milk, sugar, and agave. Sift the cocoa powder and salt and slowly add them to the cream mixture until all of the ingredients are thoroughly combined. Chill the mixture for at least 1 hour, or overnight.

Add the chilled mixture to your ice cream maker and churn it according to the manufacturer's instructions. Most machines take 10 to 15 minutes depending on the temperature of the mix, and when it's finished it should look like soft serve. Once it's churned, transfer the ice cream to a large freezer-safe container and gently fold in the brownie chunks and dark chocolate chips, being sure to maintain the air in the base. Smooth the top, cover the ice cream tightly, and freeze it for at least 5 to 6 hours or until it is firm.

Set the ice cream out for about 5 minutes to soften it before serving for optimal flavor and texture. It will keep well in the freezer for a couple of weeks in an airtight container, but is best when it's fresh.

GRAPE-NUTS® & RAISIN

Makes about 1 quart
(272 g)

· ·

2½ cups (600 ml) all-natural canned
coconut milk

⅓ cup (67 g) organic unrefined cane
sugar

¼ cup (60 ml) organic agave

1 tsp vanilla extract

½ cup (60 g) Grape-Nuts cereal

½ cup (60 g) raisins, unsweetened

When I was growing up, eating ice cream was mostly reserved for vacation, and vacation meant Maine. Almost every old-timey ice cream shop we visited there had Grape-Nuts & Raisin on its menu, and it was usually my flavor of choice. It is lightly sweet, with crazy texture thanks to the crunchy cereal and chewy raisins. It has a unique flavor that is otherwise only familiar during breakfast. I didn't even realize that Grape-Nuts & Raisin ice cream was a regional specialty until I went to college and got some pretty funny looks at the mention of it. But whether you are in Maine or Montana, this recipe is sure to become a favorite.

Use a high-speed or immersion blender or whisk to thoroughly mix the coconut milk, sugar, agave, and vanilla. Add the Grape-Nuts cereal and raisins and chill the combined mixture overnight. This will soften the cereal and raisins and infuse that yummy, nutty cereal flavor into the base.

Once the mixture is chilled, strain the cereal and raisins from the base and reserve them. Add the liquid base to your ice cream maker and churn it according to the manufacturer's instructions, or until the mixture is thick and smooth. Transfer the ice cream into a large freezer-safe container and gently fold the Grape-Nuts cereal and raisins back into it. Cover and freeze the mixture for at least 5 to 6 hours, or until it is firm.

This ice cream will keep in the freezer for a couple of weeks in an airtight container, though it is best when it's fresh.

FROM *the* BAKERY

There is nothing better than freshly baked goodies served with cool, creamy ice cream. This chapter is dedicated to ice cream flavors that eat like structured desserts. They activate all of your senses at the same time, and are sometimes unexpected but always familiar. They are the most complex to make, but by far the most popular flavors in our shops.

Almost all of the ice cream inclusions in this section are made from scratch at FoMu. It is hard to source all-natural, plant-based specialty ingredients in bulk, but it is even harder to find ones that taste great and make us feel good. I think it is important to make the components of each flavor from scratch to ensure quality and balance, but when you're in a pinch for time, feel free to substitute your favorite plant-based, all-natural, or organic store-bought ingredients.

The ratio of inclusion to ice cream in these recipes is generally pretty high. I feel strongly that ice creams with chunks should have a sturdy chunk in each and every bite. I encourage rough chopping your inclusions, as they naturally break up during mixing and dissolve a bit in the ice cream base while setting. I love tons of big irregular chunks in my ice cream. The faint of heart can certainly use less and chop more. Either way, these recipes are sure to please.

PEANUT BUTTER MUD PIE

Makes about 1 quart (272 g)

· ·

2½ cups (600 ml) all-natural canned coconut milk

¼ cup (50 g) organic unrefined cane sugar

¼ cup (60 ml) organic agave

2½ oz (70 g) natural, smooth, unsalted peanut butter, weighed and stirred

Pinch of sea salt

½ cup (84 g) Chocolate Cake (page 123), cubed

⅓ cup (75 ml) Dark Chocolate Fudge (page 136), or your favorite store-bought vegan fudge

This super indulgent ice cream is one of the most popular flavors at FoMu. It starts with a rich peanut-buttery base, and is embellished with homemade Chocolate Cake (page 123) and a Dark Chocolate Fudge swirl (page 136). It takes a few steps to make, but is worth every bit of effort. It is a sundae in a scoop!

Make sure to use a high-quality, all-natural, smooth peanut butter. You can use store-bought cake in a pinch. Day-old cake works well because it absorbs more of the cream and holds up better when folded in. You can substitute store-bought fudge as well, but a thin sauce will not maintain a prominent swirl. Add extra fudge on top for an extra muddy scoop!

Use a high-speed or immersion blender to mix the coconut milk, sugar, agave, peanut butter, and salt. Chill the mixture for at least 1 hour, or overnight.

Add the chilled mixture to your ice cream maker and churn it according to the manufacturer's instructions. Most machines take 10 to 15 minutes depending on the temperature of the mix, and it should have the consistency of soft serve when it's finished. Transfer the ice cream into a large freezer-safe container and gently add in the cake and fudge in a figure eight motion until they are evenly distributed. Do not overmix or you risk deflating the ice cream and disturbing the integrity of the cake and swirl. Transfer the ice cream to a large freezer-safe container, smooth the top, and cover it tightly. Freeze it for at least 5 to 6 hours, or until it is firm.

Set the ice cream out for 5 to 10 minutes to soften it before serving. You can store this ice cream in the freezer for up to 1 week in an airtight container, though it is best when it's fresh.

RASPBERRY ALMOND CRUMBLE

Makes about 1 quart
(272 g)

. . . .

1 pint (312 g) fresh or frozen raspberries

2 cups (480 ml) all-natural canned coconut milk

3 tbsp (37 g) organic unrefined cane sugar

¼ cup (60 ml) agave

Pinch of sea salt

¾ cup (140 g) Oatmeal Crumble (page 124) cooled to room temperature, or neutral granola

This recipe balances the sweet-yet-tart flavor of raspberry with the creaminess of coconut and the hearty crunch of oats. It is a whole classic berry crumble à la mode in one scoop. While Massachusetts is not exactly known for its bounty of fruit crops, we are especially proud of the ones we have and showcase them accordingly. My son Asher is particularly fond of raspberries: He fills his belly more than he fills his container when picking at the farm. I always use fresh, local raspberries when possible, but frozen will do in the off-season. Homemade Oatmeal Crumble (page 124) is wholesome and so simple to make, but in a pinch use your favorite store-bought neutral-flavored granola. For this recipe in particular, I like to add chopped almonds to the crumble, but that is certainly optional.

Start by making the raspberry purée. In a high-speed blender or food processor, purée the fresh or frozen red raspberries until they're smooth. Set aside ½ cup (120 ml) of the purée. Use a high-speed or immersion blender to thoroughly mix the remaining purée, coconut milk, sugar, agave, and salt. Chill the mixture for at least 1 hour, or overnight.

Add the chilled mixture to your ice cream maker and churn it according to the manufacturer's instructions. Most machines take 10 to 15 minutes depending on the temperature of the mix, and it should look like soft serve when it's finished. Transfer the churned ice cream to a large freezer-safe container. Wide and shallow containers work well for mixing, freezing, and scooping later on. Gently fold the crumbled oats into the base until they're evenly distributed. You want to be sure to maintain the air that was churned into the base for the best texture. Smooth the top, cover the container, and freeze the ice cream for at least 5 to 6 hours, or until it is set. Don't skimp on time—this ensures the best quality and shelf life of the ice cream.

For an ideal texture, set the ice cream out for 5 to 10 minutes before serving it. It will keep well in the freezer for a couple of weeks in an airtight container.

LEMON MERINGUE PIE

Lemon meringue pie is an ethereal and complex dessert, classically known for its billowing meringue top. This recipe takes all of the elements of the traditional dessert and churns them together into one stunning scoop. Fresh lemon juice makes the ice cream super bright and light, while the addition of lemon extract adds a citrus punch that balances the creamy coconut. Roughly chopped Vanilla Shortbread (page 119) and toasted marshmallows add layers of texture and sweetness without fuss.

Makes about 1 quart (272 g)

....

2 cups (480 ml) all-natural canned coconut milk

¼ cup (50 g) organic unrefined cane sugar

⅓ cup (80 ml) organic agave

½ cup (120 ml) lemon juice, freshly squeezed

½ tsp lemon extract

½ cup (25 g) all-natural, plant-based marshmallows

½ cup (25 g) Vanilla Shortbread (page 119), roughly chopped

Use a high-speed or immersion blender to mix the coconut milk, sugar, agave, lemon juice, and lemon extract. Cover and chill the mixture for at least 2 hours, or overnight.

Once the mixture is chilled, add it to your ice cream maker and churn it according to the manufacturer's instructions. Most machines take 10 to 15 minutes depending on the temperature of the mix, and when it's finished it should look like soft serve. Transfer the ice cream to a wide, freezer-safe container and gently fold in the marshmallows and shortbread until they are fairly distributed. Smooth the top and cover the ice cream tightly. Freeze it for at least 5 to 6 hours, or until it is firm.

Enjoy this ice cream fresh or store it for up to 1 week in an airtight, freezer-safe container.

BLUEBERRY SHORT-BREAD

Makes about 1 quart (272 g)

· ·

1¾ cups (440 ml) all-natural canned coconut milk

3 tbsp (37 g) organic unrefined cane sugar

⅓ cup (80 ml) organic agave

2 tbsp (30 ml) fresh lemon juice

4 oz (113 g) Vanilla Shortbread (page 119), roughly chopped

⅓ cup (80 ml) blueberry jam

Blueberries are one of the few fruits that grow locally in New England, and I picked mountains of them at the farm every year as a kid. This flavor takes this seasonal sweetheart and pairs it with a slightly tart ice cream and homemade Vanilla Shortbread (page 119) to make a scoop reminiscent of blueberry pie à la mode. It is sweet and creamy with just the right amount of texture. Summer perfection in a scoop!

Use a high-speed stand or immersion blender to thoroughly mix the coconut milk, sugar, agave, and lemon juice. Chill the mixture in a sealed container for at least 1 hour, or overnight.

Add the chilled mixture to your ice cream maker and churn it according to the manufacturer's instructions. Most machines take 10 to 15 minutes depending on the temperature of the mix, and when it's finished it should look like soft serve. Transfer the ice cream to a wide and shallow freezer-safe container and gently fold in the shortbread cookie chunks until they are evenly distributed. Then evenly pour in the blueberry jam and use a rubber spatula to make a figure eight motion to help distribute the jam without disturbing the lovely swirl too much. If you find that your jam is too thick, you can make it workable by whisking in a little water or agave. Cover and freeze the finished ice cream for at least 5 to 6 hours, or until it is firm.

Set the ice cream out for 5 to 10 minutes before serving it for an ideal texture. It will taste freshest if you keep it sealed and stored in the back of your freezer for up to 1 week.

KEY LIME PIE

Makes 1 quart (272 g)

. . . .

2 cups (480 ml) all-natural canned coconut milk

¼ cup (50 g) organic unrefined cane sugar

⅓ cup (80 ml) organic agave

½ cup (120 ml) Key or regular lime juice, freshly squeezed

½ tsp lime extract

¼ cup (25 g) shredded coconut

½ cup (25 g) Vanilla Shortbread (page 119), roughly chopped

Key limes are the smaller, yellower cousin of the traditional (Persian) lime that most of us are familiar with. They were historically grown in Key West, Florida, and are the namesake of the famous Key lime pie made there. You can use either traditional Key limes or regular limes for this recipe. More importantly, be sure to use freshly squeezed juice for the brightest, most flavorful scoop. Serve this ice cream with just a bit of lime zest for a vibrant presentation and over-the-top flavor.

Use a high-speed or immersion blender to mix the coconut milk, sugar, agave, lime juice, and lime extract. Cover and chill the mixture for at least 2 hours, or overnight.

Once the mixture is chilled, add it to your ice cream maker and churn it according to the manufacturer's instructions. Most machines take 10 to 15 minutes depending on the temperature of the mix, and when it's finished it should look like soft serve. Transfer the ice cream to a wide, freezer-safe container and gently fold in the coconut and shortbread until they are fairly distributed. Smooth the top and cover the ice cream tightly, and freeze it for at least 5 to 6 hours, or until it is firm.

This ice cream will keep well in the freezer for a couple of weeks in an airtight container.

MAGIC BAR

Makes about 1 quart
(272 g)

....

2 cups (480 ml) all-natural canned coconut milk

¼ cup (50 g) organic unrefined cane sugar

¼ cup (60 ml) organic agave

1 tbsp (15 ml) molasses

Pinch of sea salt

⅓ cup (56 g) Oatmeal Crumble (page 124), cooled to room temperature, or neutral granola

¼ cup (28 g) dark chocolate chips

¼ cup (25 g) shredded coconut

¼ cup (28 g) toasted pecans, chopped

This flavor is inspired by one of my favorite desserts of all time—7 layer bars, or "Magic Bars." I used to stockpile them from the kitchen at my college. They're traditionally made with sweetened condensed milk, butter, and graham crackers, but I cleaned the recipe up with homemade Oatmeal Crumble (page 124), toasted nuts, and coconut. The crumble is simple to make, but in a pinch, use your favorite store-bought neutral-flavored granola, graham crackers, or vanilla cookies. Freshly toasting the nuts and coconut really heightens the flavor and texture in the ice cream, and the addition of dark chocolate chips tips the dial from wholesome to decadent. Who knew my favorite college dessert would be destined for my ice cream recipe repository?

Use a high-speed or immersion blender or whisk to thoroughly mix the coconut milk, sugar, agave, molasses, and salt. Chill the mixture for at least 1 hour, or overnight.

Add the chilled mixture to your ice cream maker and churn it according to the manufacturer's instructions. Most machines take 10 to 15 minutes depending on the temperature of the mix, and when it's finished it should look like soft serve. Once it's churned, transfer the ice cream to a large, freezer-safe container. Wide and shallow containers work well for mixing, freezing, and scooping later on. Combine the crumbled oats, chocolate chips, shredded coconut, and pecans into a bowl and stir to homogenize them, then fold them into the base of the ice cream until they're evenly distributed. You want to be sure to maintain the air that was churned into the base of the ice cream for the best texture. Smooth the top and cover the ice cream tightly, and freeze it for at least 5 to 6 hours, or until it is firm.

Take the ice cream out of the freezer about 5 to 10 minutes before serving it to soften it to an ideal texture. It will taste freshest if you keep it sealed and stored in the back of your freezer for up to 1 week.

CARAMEL PECAN PIE

Makes about 1 quart
(272 g)

· ·

2 cups (480 ml) all-natural canned
coconut milk

2 tbsp (25 g) organic unrefined cane
sugar

¼ cup (50 g) Vanilla Bean Caramel
(page 139)

2 tbsp (30 ml) organic agave

Pinch of sea salt

½ cup (45 g) pecans, chopped

½ cup (25 g) Vanilla Shortbread (page
119), roughly chopped

This flavor makes an appearance every year around the holidays. It's a nod to one of my favorite Thanksgiving desserts—pecan pie à la mode. But you don't have to wait until the holidays to enjoy this pie recipe. It is simple to make and quick to come together. Vanilla Bean Caramel (page 139) infuses the base with a sweet, nutty flavor while toasted pecans and roughly chopped Vanilla Shortbread (page 119) add dimension. It is a perfectly balanced dessert that needs no adorning.

Use a high-speed or immersion blender to mix the coconut milk, sugar, caramel, agave, and salt. Cover and chill the mixture for at least 2 hours, or overnight.

Once it's chilled, add the mixture to your ice cream maker and churn it according to the manufacturer's instructions. Most machines take 10 to 15 minutes depending on the temperature of the mix, and when it's finished it should look like soft serve. Once it's churned, transfer the ice cream to a wide, freezer-safe container and gently fold in the pecans and shortbread, making sure to maintain the air in the base. Cover the ice cream tightly and freeze it for at least 5 to 6 hours, or until it is firm.

Take the ice cream out of the freezer about 5 to 10 minutes before serving it to soften it to an ideal texture. This one will keep in the freezer for a couple of weeks in an airtight container, though it is best when it's fresh.

Note: Top with Chai-Candied Pecans (page 131) for some added spice and extra texture.

SALTY HONEY-COMB

Makes about 1 quart
(272 g)

. . . .

Honeycomb candy is best described as an aerated toffee—crunchy, sweet, and slightly bitter, with an airy texture that is unique to say the least. It is a familiar favorite in Great Britain, but harder to find in the United States. Luckily for us, it is easy enough to make and wonderfully adaptable. It certainly deserves a cameo as an ice cream accompaniment. Since it is mostly comprised of sugar, the normally crunchy candy dissolves over time, leaving a slightly chewy caramel ribbon in its place. An extra sprinkling of sea salt balances the honeycomb sweetness and accentuates the toasty flavor. I highly recommend adding an extra sprinkling of honeycomb candy on top of your scoop for even more texture.

2½ cups (600 ml) all-natural canned coconut milk

¼ cup (50 g) organic unrefined cane sugar

¼ cup (60 ml) organic agave

Pinch of sea salt

1 tbsp (15 ml) pure maple syrup

½ cup (60 g) Salted Honeycomb (page 127), roughly chopped

Use a high-speed or immersion blender or whisk to thoroughly mix the coconut milk, sugar, agave, salt, and maple syrup. Chill the mixture in a sealed container for at least 1 hour, or overnight.

Once it's chilled, add the liquid base to your ice cream maker and churn it according to the manufacturer's instructions. Most machines take 10 to 15 minutes depending on the temperature of the mix, and when it's finished it should look like soft serve. Transfer the ice cream into a large, freezer-safe container and gently fold the honeycomb into the base, distributing it evenly. Cover and freeze the ice cream for at least 5 to 6 hours, or until it is firm.

Depending on the temperature of your freezer you may want to set the ice cream out for 5 to 10 minutes to soften it before serving. This ice cream will keep in the freezer for a couple of weeks in an airtight container, but it's best when fresh.

CHOCOLATE COOKIE DOUGH

Makes about 1 quart
(272 g)

Who doesn't love cookie dough? Personally, I think I like cookie dough more than I like cookies. It is chewy, sweet, and quicker to make than its baked counterpart. No ice cream menu would be complete without a cookie dough recipe. The problem with most cookie dough ice cream is that you usually only get a couple of crumb-sized pieces of the namesake ingredient, leaving you with nothing but vanilla ice cream—don't get me wrong, vanilla has its own merits, but it shouldn't replace cookie dough. This recipe is packed with big chunks of soft, sweet, homemade Salted Chocolate Chip Cookie dough (page 115). To ensure that no bite is left lacking, the base is flavored with a hint of cocoa and adorned with extra dark chocolate chunks.

2 cups (480 ml) all-natural canned coconut milk

¼ cup (50 g) organic unrefined cane sugar

¼ cup (60 ml) organic agave

1 tbsp (5 g) premium Dutch-process cocoa, weighed

¼ cup (112 g) barley malt powder

Pinch of sea salt

3 oz (84 g) dough from Salted Chocolate Chip Cookies (page 115), roughly chopped in large 1-inch (2.5-cm) cubes

2 oz (56 g) dark chocolate, chopped

Use a high-speed or immersion blender to mix the coconut milk, sugar, and agave. Whisk the cocoa, malt powder, and salt in a separate bowl until they're evenly combined. Add the dry ingredients to the coconut cream mixture and carefully blend all of the ingredients together until they are thoroughly combined. Chill the mixture for at least 1 hour, or overnight.

Add the chilled mixture to your ice cream maker and churn it according to the manufacturer's instructions. Most machines take 10 to 15 minutes depending on the temperature of the mix, and when it's finished it should look like soft serve. Once it's churned, transfer the ice cream to a large freezer-safe container and gently fold in the cookie dough chunks and chocolate, being careful to maintain the air in the base. Smooth the top and cover the ice cream tightly. Freeze it for at least 5 to 6 hours or until it is firm.

Set the ice cream out for 5 to 10 minutes to soften before serving it for optimal flavor and texture. It will keep well in the freezer for a couple of weeks in an airtight container.

FROM
Your CUP

Ice cream flavor inspiration can come from anywhere, and beverages are a wonderful source of ideas. From the bar to the café, these flavors are traditionally enjoyed by the cup, but are even better enjoyed by the scoop. Some are mature twists on childhood flavors, like Oatmeal Rum Raisin (page 57) and Bourbon Maple Walnut (page 53). Some are thought to be healing, like Golden Milk (page 65). And others are purely indulgent, like Cherry Amaretto Chunk (page 54). Enjoy these on their own, as floats, or on top of your favorite dessert. Day or night, warm or cold, holiday or workday, these recipes will hit the spot.

BOURBON MAPLE WALNUT

Makes about 1 quart
(272 g)

. . . .

2½ cups (600 ml) all-natural canned coconut milk

¼ cup (50 g) organic unrefined cane sugar

3 tbsp (45 ml) pure maple syrup

2 tbsp (30 ml) triple-aged bourbon (optional)

Pinch of sea salt

2 oz (56 g) chopped walnuts, plus more for serving

Maple has always been one of my favorite flavors. It is aromatic, nutty, and versatile— there really is no substitute for pure maple syrup. Living in New England, I was fortunate to grow up around maple farms and celebrate all things maple, from candies to pancakes to ice cream, naturally. This recipe is a kicked-up version of a classic maple walnut ice cream. The bourbon is optional, but makes the base extra smooth. Maple syrup may not be local to you, but 100 percent real syrup is a must. It is the star ingredient in the recipe and quality makes all the difference!

Use a high-speed or immersion blender to mix the coconut milk, sugar, maple syrup, bourbon, if you're using it, and salt. Chill the mixture for at least 2 hours, or overnight.

Once the mixture has chilled, add it to your ice cream maker and churn it according to the manufacturer's instructions. Most machines take 10 to 15 minutes depending on the temperature of the mix, and when it's finished it should look like soft serve. Once the ice cream is churned, transfer it to a large freezer-safe container and gently fold in the walnuts. Smooth the top and cover it tightly. Freeze it for at least 5 to 6 hours, or until it is firm.

The ice cream will be softer set with the bourbon than without. This ice cream will keep in the freezer for a couple of weeks in an airtight container, but it's best when fresh. Top with extra walnuts, if desired.

CHERRY AMARETTO CHUNK

It's no secret—cherries and dark chocolate have long been best friends. The rich and slightly bitter dark chocolate marries so well with the sweet and bold red cherry. This recipe uses puréed and chopped cherries to enhance the flavor and texture of the ice cream. You can use frozen cherries in a pinch, but fresh cherries make this ice cream out of this world. Feel free to omit the amaretto if you prefer, but be sure to use a high-quality dark chocolate—it makes a huge difference!

Makes about 1 quart (272 g)

....

2 cups (300 g) fresh or frozen red cherries, pitted

2 tbsp (30 ml) amaretto liquor (optional)

1¾ cups (420 ml) all-natural canned coconut milk

⅓ cup (67 g) organic unrefined cane sugar

2 tbsp (30 ml) organic agave

Pinch of sea salt

½ cup (125 g) dark chocolate, roughly chopped

Use a food processor to purée half of the cherries. Roughly chop the remaining cherries, and if you're using amaretto pour it over them to soak. Set the chopped cherries aside.

Use a high-speed or immersion blender to mix the cherry purée, coconut milk, sugar, agave, and salt. Chill the mixture for at least 2 hours, or overnight.

Once the mixture is chilled, add it to your ice cream maker and churn it according to the manufacturer's instructions. Most machines take 10 to 15 minutes depending on the temperature of the mix, and when it's finished it should look like soft serve. Once it's churned, transfer the ice cream to a wide, freezer-safe container and gently fold in the chopped cherries and dark chocolate. Smooth the top, cover the ice cream tightly, and freeze it for at least 5 to 6 hours, or until it is firm.

Depending on the temperature of your freezer, you may want to set the ice cream out for 5 to 10 minutes to soften it before serving. Store it in an airtight, freezer-safe container for up to 1 week.

OATMEAL RUM RAISIN

Makes about 1 quart
(272 g)

. . . .

2½ cups (600 ml) all-natural canned coconut milk

¼ cup (50 g) organic unrefined cane sugar

¼ cup (60 ml) organic agave

1 tsp ground cinnamon

2 tbsp (30 ml) dark rum (optional)

⅔ cup (75 g) Oatmeal Crumble (page 124), or neutral granola

⅓ cup (50 g) unsweetened raisins

This flavor is a hybrid of two dessert classics—the oatmeal raisin cookie and rum raisin ice cream. This sweet, spiked, and spiced ice cream has something for everyone. It has a wonderfully hearty texture, thanks to homemade Oatmeal Crumble (page 124) and soaked raisins. If you are avoiding alcohol, you are welcome to omit the rum, but it may alter the texture of the ice cream just a bit.

Use a high-speed or immersion blender to mix the coconut milk, sugar, agave, cinnamon, and rum, if you're using it. Cover and chill the mixture for at least 2 hours, or overnight.

Once it is chilled, add the mixture to your ice cream maker and churn it according to the manufacturer's instructions. Most machines take 10 to 15 minutes depending on the temperature of the mix, and when it's finished it should look like soft serve. Once it's churned, transfer the ice cream to a wide, freezer-safe container and fold in the oatmeal crumble and raisins, making sure to maintain the air in the base. Cover the ice cream tightly and freeze it for at least 5 to 6 hours, or until it is firm.

Store this ice cream in an airtight container in the freezer for up to 1 week.

CHOCOLATE STOUT

Makes about 1 quart
(272 g)

....

Stout is a dark beer that includes roasted malt or barley, hops, and yeast. It may sound odd as an ice cream flavor, but it is a particularly good match for a couple of reasons: Stouts, especially milk or chocolate stouts, have a rich, deep flavor that marries nicely with chocolate and cream, and the alcohol in stout gives ice cream a smoother, softer texture that helps to ward off crystallization. This recipe calls for reducing your favorite stout to concentrate the flavor and ensure the ice cream does not get too icy. Use a high-quality Dutch-process cocoa for a rich flavor that complements the bitter stout, and top this one with some hot fudge or a sprinkle of Toasty Coconut (page 128) for added texture.

1 cup (240 ml) milk stout or chocolate stout

2 cups (480 ml) all-natural canned coconut milk

¼ cup (50 g) organic unrefined cane sugar

2 tbsp (30 ml) organic agave

1 tbsp (15 ml) molasses

1 oz (28 g) premium Dutch-process cocoa, weighed

Pinch of sea salt

In a small saucepan, simmer the stout over medium heat until it is reduced by half, about 20 minutes, leaving ½ cup (120 ml) of concentrated stout. Let it cool to room temperature.

Use a high-speed or immersion blender to mix the concentrated stout, coconut milk, sugar, agave, molasses, cocoa, and salt. Pour into a container, cover, and chill the mixture for at least 2 hours, or overnight.

Once the mixture is chilled, add it to your ice cream maker and churn it according to the manufacturer's instructions. Most machines take 10 to 15 minutes depending on the temperature of the mix, and when it's finished it should look like soft serve. Once it's churned, transfer the ice cream to a large, freezer-safe container, smooth the top, and cover it tightly. Freeze it for at least 5 to 6 hours or until it is firm.

Store this ice cream in the freezer in a sealed, airtight container for up to 1 week.

EARL GREY SHORT-BREAD

Makes 1 quart (272 g)

. . . .

2 Earl Grey tea bags or 2 tbsp (4 g) of loose leaf tea

½ cup (120 ml) hot water

2¼ cups (520 ml) all-natural canned coconut milk

⅓ cup (67 g) unrefined cane sugar

¼ cup (60 ml) agave

Pinch of salt

¾ cup (112 g) Vanilla Shortbread (page 119), roughly chopped

One of my favorite drinks is a London Fog, also known as an Earl Grey Latte. I like it so much that I brew it in bulk and store it to serve hot or over ice with almond milk. The warm, aromatic flavor of bergamot makes you feel good—and even a little regal! Use a good-quality Earl Grey tea and add a couple of drops of bergamot oil if you want an extra oomph. This ice cream pairs perfectly with our simple yet sweet Vanilla Shortbread (page 119) or even store-bought biscotti. You might even find yourself nibbling on it for breakfast. No judgment!

Start by making the tea concentrate. Steep the Earl Grey tea in ½ cup (120 ml) of hot water. Let it steep for twice the recommended amount of time. The reduced water ensures less iciness in the finished ice cream, while the extra tea and steep time ensures full flavor. Discard the teabags and let the tea cool to room temperature.

Use a high-speed or immersion blender or whisk to thoroughly mix the tea, coconut milk, sugar, agave, and salt. Chill the mixture in a sealed container for at least 1 hour, or overnight.

Add the chilled mixture to your ice cream maker and churn it according to the manufacturer's instructions. Most machines take 10 to 15 minutes depending on the temperature of the mix, and when it's finished it should look like soft serve. Once it's churned, transfer the ice cream to a large, freezer-safe container. Wide and shallow containers work well for mixing, freezing, and scooping later on. Gently fold the shortbread chunks into the base until they're evenly distributed, making sure to maintain the air that was churned into the base for the best texture. Smooth the top, cover, and freeze the finished ice cream for at least 5 to 6 hours, or until it is firm.

This ice cream is best served fresh, but it can be stored in an airtight container in the freezer for up to 1 week.

MATCHA WHITE CHOCOLATE

Matcha is a unique variation of Japanese green tea. It is shade-grown to develop its flavor and ground to a powder to allow it to dissolve more readily in liquids. Lattes have become a popular way to consume matcha, as the creamy milk mellows the earthy and vegetal quality of the vibrant green and uniquely flavorful matcha. This recipe takes the matcha latte to the next level with the creamy and exotic addition of coconut and the sweet crunch of white chocolate throughout.

Makes 1 quart (272 g)

....

2½ cups (600 ml) all-natural canned coconut milk

¼ cup (50 g) organic unrefined cane sugar

⅓ cup (80 ml) agave

½ oz (14 g) matcha powder

Pinch of sea salt

2½ oz (70 g) vegan white chocolate chips

Use a high-speed or immersion blender to thoroughly mix the coconut milk, sugar, agave, matcha, and salt. Chill the mixture in a sealed container for at least 1 hour, or overnight.

Add the chilled mixture to your ice cream maker and churn it according to the manufacturer's instructions. Most machines take 10 to 15 minutes depending on the temperature of the mix, and when it's finished it should look like soft serve. Once it's churned, transfer the ice cream to a wide, shallow, freezer-safe container and gently fold the white chocolate chips into the base until they're evenly distributed, making sure to maintain the air that was churned into the base. Smooth the top, cover, and freeze the finished ice cream for at least 5 to 6 hours, or until it is firm. If the ice cream does not fully set, it will compromise the quality over time.

Serve this ice cream fresh, or store it in an airtight container in the freezer for up to 1 week.

GOLDEN MILK

Makes about 1 quart
(272 g)

For those who haven't yet been dazzled by this trendy drink, it is exotic, delicious, and great for you. Inspired by a traditional Indian tea, this beautifully vibrant yellow drink includes ginger, turmeric, and cinnamon, all known for their anti-inflammatory and antiseptic qualities. This ice cream recipe contains all of the elements of the famed drink in a cool, creamy scoop. The addition of finely diced crystallized ginger adds flavor and lovely shimmering chunks to every scoop.

. . . .

2 oz (56 g) ginger root, finely diced

2 oz (56 g) turmeric root, finely diced

½ cup (100 g) organic unrefined cane sugar

½ cup (120 ml) water

2½ cups (600 ml) all-natural canned coconut milk

1 tbsp (15 ml) organic agave

Pinch of sea salt

¼ tsp black pepper, finely ground

½ tsp ground cinnamon

½ cup (125 g) candied ginger, finely diced

Place the ginger, turmeric, sugar, and water in a saucepan and cook them over low heat for 10 minutes. Turn off the heat and let the mixture cool to room temperature. Press it through a fine-mesh sieve, discard the ginger root, and reserve the syrup. Set it aside.

Use a high-speed or immersion blender to mix the turmeric-ginger syrup, coconut milk, agave, salt, black pepper, and cinnamon. Chill the mixture for at least 2 hours, or overnight.

Once the mixture is chilled, add it to your ice cream maker and churn it according to the manufacturer's instructions. Most machines take 10 to 15 minutes depending on the temperature of the mix, and when it's finished it should look like soft serve. Once it's churned, transfer the ice cream to a wide, freezer-safe container, and gently fold in the candied ginger. Smooth the top, cover the ice cream tightly, and freeze it for at least 5 to 6 hours, or until it is firm.

Depending on the temperature of your freezer, you may want to set the ice cream out for 5 to 10 minutes to soften it before serving. This ice cream will keep in the freezer for a couple of weeks in an airtight container, but it's best when fresh.

COLD BREW

Makes 1 quart (272 g)

. . . .

⅓ cup (60 g) medium-ground coffee beans

2½ cups (600 ml) all-natural canned coconut milk

¼ cup (50 g) organic unrefined cane sugar

¼ cup (60 ml) agave

1 tbsp (15 ml) pure vanilla extract

Pinch of sea salt

Coffee ice cream is one of those flavors I normally would glaze right over. Don't get me wrong, I LOVE my coffee, but I'd never tasted a coffee ice cream I was jazzed about—until this recipe. This recipe uses your favorite real, cold-brewed coffee, concentrated to infuse extra flavor and reduce iciness. So use coffee you would drink—it's the star of the show. If you're not a coffee ice cream fan, this recipe might just change your mind.

In a bowl, combine the coffee grounds and coconut milk. Cover this mixture and place it in the refrigerator to steep overnight, at least 12 hours or more. Once it's steeped, use a fine-mesh strainer to remove the grounds from the coconut milk. If you find that your coconut milk has separated and there is a layer of cream on top, stir it and let the milk warm enough to homogenize before straining it. Discard the grounds.

Use a high-speed or immersion blender to mix the coconut milk coffee, sugar, agave, vanilla, and salt.

Add the mixture to your ice cream maker and churn it according to the manufacturer's instructions. Most machines take 10 to 15 minutes depending on the temperature of the mix, and when it's finished it should look like soft serve. Once it's churned, transfer the ice cream to a large freezer-safe container, smooth the top, and cover it tightly. Freeze the finished ice cream for at least 5 to 6 hours, or until it is firm.

Store this ice cream in the freezer in a sealed container for up to 1 week.

Note: For a coffee-holic's dream, top your favorite iced or hot coffee or espresso with a scoop of Cold Brew ice cream. The sweetness and richness are perfect complements.

COOKIES & 'NOG

Makes about 1 quart
(272 g)

....

2 cups (480 ml) all-natural canned
coconut milk

1 tbsp (14 g) unrefined cane sugar

2 tbsp (28 g) light brown sugar

⅓ cup (80 ml) agave

2 tbsp (30 ml) whiskey or bourbon
(optional)

½ tsp nutmeg

Pinch of sea salt

¾ cup (112 g) Vanilla Shortbread (page
119), roughly chopped

Eggnog is a time-honored holiday drink that I've always loved the idea of, but never made. Traditionally composed of heavy cream and raw egg, it is intimidating to make and even more intimidating to drink. This recipe takes all of the deliciously festive elements of eggnog and churns them into a simple, egg-free scoop. The addition of homemade Vanilla Shortbread (page 119) adds flavor, texture, and composition. Feel free to omit the alcohol if you are steering clear, but it won't taste as traditional. Now you can toast to a new holiday dessert!

Use a high-speed or immersion blender to thoroughly mix the coconut milk, sugars, agave, whiskey, if you're using it, nutmeg, and salt. Chill the mixture in a sealed container for at least 1 hour, or overnight.

Add the chilled mixture to your ice cream maker and churn it according to the manufacturer's instructions. Most machines take 10 to 15 minutes depending on the temperature of the mix, and when it's finished it should look like soft serve. Once it's churned, transfer the ice cream to a freezer-safe container. Wide and shallow containers work well for mixing, freezing, and scooping later on. Gently fold the shortbread chunks into the base until they are evenly distributed, making sure to maintain the air that was churned into the base. Smooth the top, cover the finished ice cream, and freeze it for at least 5 to 6 hours, or until it is firm. If the ice cream does not fully set, it will compromise the quality over time.

Depending on the temperature of your freezer, you may want to set the ice cream out for 5 to 10 minutes to soften it before serving. Store this ice cream in an airtight container for up to 1 week.

AT *the* MARKET

I grew up picking fruits and veggies from our local farm and farmers' markets every Sunday, almost religiously, from the start of spring until late fall. That tradition created some of my most favorite memories. My dad would bite into peppers and tomatoes like they were apples, and we would fill our baskets and our bellies with produce so delicious it needed no preparation. Those memories and flavors have shaped the way I eat and the way I raise my kids today.

The following ice cream recipes celebrate Earth's bounty, whether local or exotic. In New England, our local crops are limited and growing seasons are short, so when I have the opportunity to use local produce, I take it. Depending on where you live and what is in season, choose fresh and choose local whenever you're able. It always tastes better. It is also a great way to enjoy in-season produce all winter long! Otherwise, head to your favorite market and look for the ripest organic produce you can find. The riper the avocados, berries, and bananas, the bolder their ice cream flavor. Starting with great ingredients means ending with great ice cream.

AVOCADO LIME

Makes about 1 quart
(272 g)

. . . .

2 cups (480 ml) all-natural canned
coconut milk

⅓ cup (67 g) organic unrefined cane
sugar

¼ cup (60 ml) organic agave

1 whole avocado, diced

2 tbsp (30 ml) lime juice (the juice of
about 1 lime)

Pinch of sea salt

Avocado ice cream? Yep. It has been a signature flavor at FoMu since day one. And although it's become a little less obscure through the general popularity of avocado and the endorsement of a notable athlete, we still get the same curious questions when newbies first see it on the menu. Smooth and slightly tangy, this mellow scoop is a refreshing treat on a hot day, and it's an amazing addition to your daily smoothie. Use whole, extra-ripe, freshly cut Haas avocados for the best flavor. Freshly squeezed lime juice brightens the flavor and keeps the ice cream a vibrant green.

Use a high-speed or immersion blender to thoroughly mix all of the ingredients until they are completely smooth. Chill the mixture for at least 1 hour, or overnight.

Add the chilled mixture to your ice cream maker and churn it according to the manufacturer's instructions. Most machines take 10 to 15 minutes depending on the temperature of the mix, and when it's finished it should look like soft serve. Once it's churned, transfer the ice cream to a large, freezer-safe container. Smooth the top, cover, and freeze it for at least 5 to 6 hours, or until it is firm.

Depending on the temperature of your freezer, you may want to set the ice cream out for 5 to 10 minutes to soften it before serving. This ice cream will keep in the freezer for a couple of weeks in an airtight container, though it is best when it's fresh.

CANDIED SWEET POTATO

Makes about 1 quart
(272 g)

. . . .

2 raw sweet potatoes

2¼ cups (540 ml) all-natural canned coconut milk

2 tbsp (25 g) organic unrefined cane sugar

2 tbsp (24 g) organic light brown sugar

2 tbsp (30 ml) organic agave

2 tbsp (30 ml) pure maple syrup

Pinch of sea salt

½ cup (25 g) all-natural, plant-based marshmallows

¼ cup (25 g) pecans, chopped

Sweet potatoes are generally available year-round, but their peak season ranges from late October through December. Sweet potato casserole is a traditional holiday preparation of these bright orange beauties, made with toasted marshmallows and pecans. Source local sweet potatoes when possible, and always look for bright orange, blemish-free spuds. You will want to look for all-natural, vegan marshmallows because they stay chewy when frozen and don't contain gelatin. As always, choose 100 percent pure maple syrup, no exceptions. This may just be a new staple on your holiday dessert table!

Preheat your oven to 350°F (177°C). Lightly grease a baking sheet with a neutral oil, such as coconut oil or canola oil. Peel and chop the sweet potatoes and lay them in an even layer on the baking sheet. Bake them for 30 to 40 minutes, or until the potatoes are fork tender and golden. Once they're cool, use a food processor or fork to purée them. Set aside 1 cup (150 g) of the sweet potato purée.

Use a high-speed or immersion blender to mix the coconut milk, sugars, agave, and maple syrup.

Add the puréed potato and salt, and blend until the mixture is completely smooth. Chill it for at least 2 hours, or overnight.

Once it's chilled, add the mixture to your ice cream maker and churn according to the manufacturer's instructions. Most machines take 10 to 15 minutes depending on the temperature of the mix, and when it's finished it should look like soft serve. Once it's churned, transfer the ice cream to a large, freezer-safe container and gently fold in the marshmallows and pecans. Smooth the top, cover the ice cream tightly, and freeze it for at least 5 to 6 hours, or until it is firm.

You can store this ice cream in the freezer in a sealed container for up to 1 week.

SWEET LAVENDER

Makes about 1 quart
(272 g)

. . . .

2¼ cups (540 ml) all-natural canned coconut milk

⅓ cup (67 g) organic unrefined cane sugar

¼ cup (60 ml) organic agave

3 tbsp (40 g) dried edible lavender flowers, plus more for serving

Pinch of sea salt

¼ cup (60 ml) purple carrot juice (optional) (You can find this online, or in many specialty food stores.)

Lavender is one of those flavors that people either love or hate. I am in the love camp, but only if it is done just right. Lavender is a lovely little purple flower that is richly floral in flavor and scent. If done poorly, it tastes like soap. If done right, it tastes like heaven. In this recipe I use real, dried lavender flower to avoid a fake soapy taste. The ice cream base is naturally white, but you can add a touch of purple carrot juice for a lovely pop of color. This delicate and sweet flavor is a unique and elegant option to have in your ice cream recipe repertoire.

Combine the coconut milk, sugar, agave, lavender, and salt in a 2-quart (2-L) heavy saucepan over medium heat. Bring the mixture to a boil, stirring it occasionally, then remove the pan from heat. Let it steep, covered, for 30 minutes.

Once it's steeped, pour the cream mixture through a fine-mesh sieve into a bowl and discard the lavender flowers. Whisk in the purple carrot juice, if you're using it. Cover and chill the mixture for at least 2 hours, or overnight.

Add the chilled mixture to your ice cream maker and churn it according to the manufacturer's instructions. Most machines take 10 to 15 minutes depending on the temperature of the mix, and when it's finished it should look like soft serve. Transfer the churned ice cream to a large freezer-safe container. Smooth the top, cover the ice cream, and freeze it for at least 5 to 6 hours or until it is firm.

Serve this ice cream decorated with lavender flower for an extra special presentation. You can store this one in a sealed container in the freezer for up to 1 week.

ROASTED BANANA CINNAMON

In my opinion, banana has long been underrated, misunderstood, and mistreated. It is versatile, sweet, and flavorful, but has historically been misrepresented by artificial flavor and yellow #5. This recipe uses roasted bananas to add sweetness, robust flavor, and amazing texture. The simple addition of cinnamon adds depth and character. This also makes a super yummy popsicle if you pour the base into wide popsicle molds instead of churning it. Dust the tops with extra cinnamon for a sweet touch of extra flavor.

Makes about 1 quart
(272 g)

. . . .

3 bananas

2 cups (480 ml) all-natural canned coconut milk

⅓ cup (67 g) organic unrefined cane sugar

2 tbsp (30 ml) organic agave

½ tsp ground cinnamon

Pinch of sea salt

Preheat your oven to 375°F (190°C). Lightly grease a baking sheet with a neutral-flavored oil, such as coconut oil or canola oil. Peel the bananas, slice them in half lengthwise, and lay them in an even layer on the baking sheet. Bake for 30 minutes, or until the banana slices are golden and sticky. Once they're cool, use a food processor or fork to purée them. You should end up with around 1 cup (225 g) of purée; set this aside.

Use a high-speed or immersion blender to mix the coconut milk, sugar, and agave. Add the puréed banana, cinnamon, and salt, and blend until the mixture is completely smooth. Chill it for at least 2 hours, or overnight.

Once the mixture is chilled, add it to your ice cream maker and churn it according to the manufacturer's instructions. Most machines take 10 to 15 minutes depending on the temperature of the mix, and when it's finished it should look like soft serve. Once it is churned, transfer the ice cream to a large, freezer-safe container, smooth the top, and cover it tightly. Freeze the ice cream for at least 5 to 6 hours, or until it is firm.

You can store this ice cream for up to 1 week in the freezer in a sealed container.

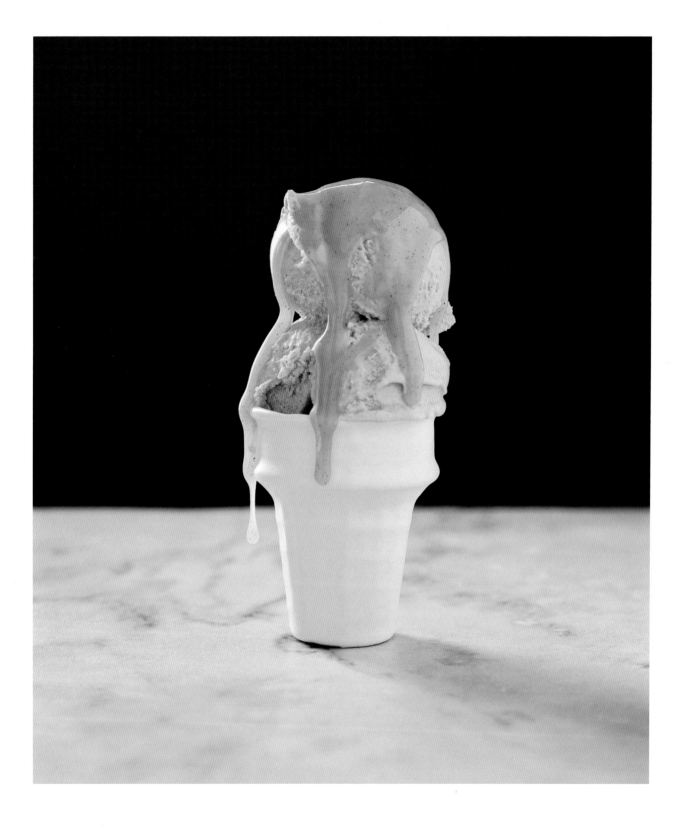

PUMPKIN CARAMEL

Makes about 1 quart
(272 g)

* *

Pumpkin season in New England is pretty epic. You can find a pumpkin version of almost anything—from cereal to coffee to muffins. Unfortunately, many of these items aren't made with pumpkin at all. Artificial flavors and colors have replaced real pumpkin to save money and time. This recipe pays homage to my mom, who always uses freshly roasted sugar pumpkin in her holiday pies and inspired me to do the same. You can substitute with kabocha or butternut squash, just make sure your winter squash of choice is fresh. Trust me—you will never think of pumpkin the same way again!

1 small sugar pumpkin or starchy
winter squash

1¾ cups (420 ml) all-natural canned
coconut milk

½ cup (50 g) organic unrefined cane
sugar

2 tbsp (30 ml) pure maple syrup

½ tsp cinnamon

Pinch of sea salt

⅓ cup (80 ml) Vanilla Bean Caramel
(page 139), or your favorite store-
bought caramel

Preheat your oven to 375°F (190°C). Lightly grease a baking sheet with a neutral-flavored oil, such as coconut oil or canola oil. Peel, deseed, and cube your sugar pumpkin. Lay the cubes in an even layer on the baking sheet and bake for 30 to 40 minutes, or until they're golden and fork tender. Once they're cool, use a food processor or fork to purée them. Set aside 1 cup (225 g) of the purée.

Use a high-speed or immersion blender to mix the coconut milk, sugar, and maple syrup. Add the puréed squash, cinnamon, and salt, and blend until the mixture is completely smooth. Chill it for at least 2 hours, or overnight.

Once it's chilled, add the mixture to your ice cream maker and churn it according to the manufacturer's instructions. Most machines take 10 to 15 minutes depending on the temperature of the mix, and when it's finished it should look like soft serve. Once it's churned, transfer the ice cream to a wide, shallow, freezer-safe container, and gently stir in the caramel in a figure eight motion. Do not over stir or you will lose the ripple and be left with a very soft set ice cream. Cover the ice cream tightly and freeze it for at least 5 to 6 hours, or until it is firm.

This ice cream will keep in the freezer for a couple of weeks in an airtight container, but it's best when fresh.

Note: Sprinkling Spiced Pepitas (page 135) onto a warm flavor such as Pumpkin Caramel or Golden Milk (page 65) intensifies the spices and adds a welcomed crunch!

FRESH STRAW-BERRY

Strawberry is a classic flavor you can find on just about any ice cream menu. But new customers who try FoMu strawberry ice cream often say "this is the best strawberry ice cream I've ever had!" It just might be, and for good reason—we use tons of real strawberries, and preserve some of their texture in the process. Making ice cream with fresh strawberries may require more time and money, but it is worth every cent. Use fresh, in-season berries whenever possible, but in a pinch, frozen will do just fine.

Makes about 1 quart (272 g)

. . . .

2 cups (400 g) fresh strawberries, puréed with some chunks remaining

2 cups (480 ml) all-natural canned coconut milk

¼ cup (50 g) organic unrefined cane sugar

5 tbsp (75 ml) organic agave

1 tsp lemon juice

Use a high-speed or immersion blender to mix the strawberry purée, coconut milk, sugar, agave, and lemon juice. Cover and chill the mixture for at least 2 hours, or overnight.

Once it's chilled, add the mixture to your ice cream maker and churn according to the manufacturer's instructions. Most machines take 10 to 15 minutes depending on the temperature of the mix, and when it's finished it should look like soft serve. Once it's churned, transfer the ice cream to a large, freezer-safe container, smooth the top and cover it tightly. Freeze it for at least 5 to 6 hours, or until it is firm.

Store this ice cream in the freezer in an airtight container for up to 1 week.

FRESH MINT CHUNK

Makes about 1 quart
(272 g)

. . . .

½ cup (100 g) packed fresh mint leaves

½ cup (100 g) organic unrefined cane sugar

¼ cup (60 ml) water

2 cups (480 ml) all-natural canned coconut milk

1 tbsp (15 ml) organic agave

½ tsp peppermint oil (optional)

¾ cup (112 g) dark chocolate, roughly chopped

You have probably seen mint chocolate chip, in all of its bright green glory, on just about every ice cream shop menu. This recipe is a little different. It has no artificial color and calls for fresh mint leaves instead of mint flavoring. The mint leaves are cooked down into a syrup and added to the base for a refreshing, herbal-tasting mint ice cream. Most mint varieties will work, but the flavor may vary slightly, so feel free to experi-mint!

In a small saucepan, simmer the fresh mint, cane sugar, and water over medium heat until it is slightly reduced, for about 7 minutes. You should be left with about ⅔ cup (160 ml) of concentrated mint syrup. Let the syrup cool to room temperature, then pass it through a fine-mesh sieve, making sure to squeeze out all of the syrup from the mint leaves. Discard the mint leaves.

Use a high-speed or immersion blender to mix the mint syrup, coconut milk, agave, and peppermint oil, if you're using it. Chill the mixture for at least 2 hours, or overnight. This will give the base an opportunity to perfume and come to a better churning temperature.

Add the chilled mixture to your ice cream maker and churn it according to the manufacturer's instructions. When the base has the consistency of a thick milkshake, transfer the ice cream to a shallow, wide, freezer-safe container, and fold in the dark chocolate chunks. Smooth the top of the ice cream and cover it tightly. Freeze it for at least 5 to 6 hours, or until it is firm.

Store this ice cream in the freezer in an airtight container for up to 1 week.

APPLE CIDER DONUT

Makes about 1 quart
(272 g)

· ·

1 cup (240 ml) apple cider (local, if available)

2 cups (480 ml) all-natural canned coconut milk

¼ cup (50 g) organic unrefined cane sugar

2 tbsp (30 ml) agave

1 tsp ground cinnamon

½ tsp ground nutmeg

¾ cup (40 g) cider donut, plain donut, or spiced vegan cake, roughly chopped

In a small saucepan, simmer the

There are few times more cherished in New England than apple season. Fall is never complete without a visit to your local orchard, some fresh apple cider, waaaay too many apples, and almost as many apple cider donuts. This recipe summons all of the nostalgia of the farm, without the hayride. If apple cider is not in season, feel free to substitute apple juice, although the flavor will be slightly different.

apple cider over medium heat for about 10 minutes or until it is reduced by half. You should be left with ½ cup (120 ml) of concentrated cider. Let it cool to room temperature.

Use a high-speed or immersion blender to mix the concentrated cider, coconut milk, sugar, agave, cinnamon, and nutmeg. Chill the mixture for at least 2 hours, or overnight.

Add the chilled mixture to your ice cream maker and churn it according to the manufacturer's instructions. Most machines take 10 to 15 minutes depending on the temperature of the mix, and when it's finished it should look like soft serve. Once it's churned, transfer the ice cream to a shallow, wide, freezer-safe container, and gently fold in the donut or cake chunks, making sure to maintain the air churned into the base. Smooth the top and cover the ice cream tightly. Freeze it for at least 5 to 6 hours, or until it is firm.

Store this ice cream in the freezer in an airtight container for up to 1 week.

STRAW-BERRY RHUBARB PIE

Makes about 1 quart
(272 g)

. . . .

1 cup (150 g) fresh rhubarb, trimmed
and diced

⅓ cup (67 g) organic unrefined cane
sugar

½ tsp lemon juice

1¾ cups (420 ml) all-natural canned
coconut milk

⅓ cup (75 g) fresh strawberries, puréed

¼ cup (60 ml) organic agave

¾ cup (45 g) Vanilla Shortbread (page
119), roughly chopped

Rhubarb is one of the first crops of the season in New England. This naturally tart, celery-looking vegetable is generally sweetened and showcased in pies and jams. Strawberry-rhubarb pie is sweet, tart, and commonly served à la mode to add a cool, creamy richness. This recipe similarly highlights fresh rhubarb and strawberries, and uses homemade shortbread for another layer of sweetness and texture. It is a must-make to kick off spring. Churn an extra batch while the ingredients are fresh and in season.

Place the diced rhubarb, sugar, and lemon juice in a small saucepan and simmer them over medium heat for 8 to 10 minutes. Remove it from heat and let it cool to room temperature, then set it aside.

Use a high-speed or immersion blender to mix the cooled rhubarb mixture, coconut milk, strawberry purée, and agave. Cover and chill the mixture for at least 2 hours, or overnight.

Once the mixture is chilled, add it to your ice cream maker and churn it according to the manufacturer's instructions. Most machines take 10 to 15 minutes depending on the temperature of the mix, and when it's finished it should look like soft serve. Once it's churned, transfer the ice cream to a wide, freezer-safe container and fold in the shortbread chunks, making sure to maintain the air churned into the base. Cover the ice cream tightly and freeze it for at least 5 to 6 hours, or until it is firm.

Store this ice cream in the freezer in an airtight container for up to 1 week.

BROWN SUGAR CORN

Makes about 1 quart
(272 g)

· ·

1 cup (175 g) corn, fresh or frozen

1¾ cups (420 ml) all-natural canned coconut milk

2 tbsp (25 g) organic unrefined cane sugar

2 tbsp (28 g) organic brown sugar

2 tbsp (30 ml) organic agave

2 tbsp (30 ml) pure maple syrup

½ tsp vanilla extract

Pinch of sea salt

Fresh corn is sweet and almost milky in texture. When I was in college, I would drive by a local cornfield, snag a fresh ear of corn, and eat it raw then and there. It is delicious on its own and makes an amazing ice cream flavor. Steeping real corn into the base of the ice cream adds texture and a uniquely fresh flavor. Fresh corn is best, especially when it is local and in season, but don't hesitate to substitute frozen if it isn't accessible. Brown sugar and maple syrup add depth of flavor and an additional hint of sweetness to this recipe.

Purée the corn in a small food processor until it has the consistency of applesauce. Set 1 cup (240 ml) aside.

Bring the coconut milk, sugars, agave, maple syrup, vanilla, and salt to a simmer in a 2-quart (2-L) heavy saucepan over medium heat, and then add the corn purée. Bring the mixture back to a simmer for 5 minutes, then remove the pan from heat and let it steep, covered, for 30 minutes to 1 hour. Pour the cream mixture through a fine-mesh sieve into a bowl and discard any large corn remnants. Cover and chill the mixture for at least 2 hours, or overnight.

Add the chilled mixture to your ice cream maker and churn it according to the manufacturer's instructions. Most machines take 10 to 15 minutes depending on the temperature of the mix, and when it's finished it should look like soft serve. Transfer the churned ice cream to a large, freezer-safe container, smooth the top, cover, and freeze it for at least 5 to 6 hours, or until it is firm.

Store this ice cream in the freezer in an airtight container for up to 1 week.

AROUND
the GLOBE

My favorite way to celebrate culture is through food, and so my diverse travels have always served as glorified food tours. This chapter showcases some of my favorite global flavors in ice cream form.

While I didn't appreciate it at the time, I was brought up eating a lot of ethnic food. I am of Middle Eastern descent, and my default flavor repertoire is certainly Mediterranean-inspired. Ice creams in this chapter like Rosewater Saffron (page 107) and Cardamom Pistachio (page 100) celebrate those flavors that I grew up eating.

After I met my husband, who is of Chinese descent, I became pretty obsessed with Asian ingredients. He would impatiently wait for me to look at almost every item in the Asian market near our house, and smirk as I asked questions like a kid in grade school. These newfound flavor combinations and ingredients inspired flavors in this section like Thai Tea (page 103), Black Sesame (page 111) and Thai Chili Peanut (page 95).

You will also find some familiar global dessert favorites, such as Tiramisu (page 108) and Banoffee Pie (page 104), in a less familiar format. Unpack your ice cream machine and explore this world of exotic ice cream flavors.

THAI CHILI PEANUT

Makes 1 quart (272 g)

. . . .

2¾ cups (660 ml) all-natural canned coconut milk

⅓ cup (67 g) organic unrefined cane sugar

3 tbsp (45 ml) organic agave

2 tbsp (32 g) all-natural creamy peanut butter

2 tsp (10 ml) lime juice

1 tsp Thai chili powder or cayenne pepper

¼ cup (30 g) peanuts, shelled and roasted

¼ cup (25 g) shredded coconut

Yep. You read that correctly. This flavor is inspired by my love of Thai food. You know that yummy peanut sauce that comes with a variety of dishes on Thai menus? It is my condiment of choice for almost everything, and this recipe offers the same sweet, nutty flavors in a cool, creamy scoop with a touch of spice. It is unique, textural, and flavorful. Feel free to remove the chili altogether or turn it up or down based on your taste.

Use a high-speed or immersion blender to mix the coconut milk, sugar, agave, peanut butter, lime juice, and chili powder. Cover and chill the mixture for at least 2 hours, or overnight.

Once the mixture is chilled, add it to your ice cream maker and churn it according to the manufacturer's instructions. Most machines take 10 to 15 minutes depending on the temperature of the mix, and when it's finished it should look like soft serve. Once it's churned, transfer the ice cream to a wide, freezer-safe container and fold in the peanuts and coconut, making sure to maintain the air that was churned into the base. Cover the ice cream tightly and freeze it for at least 5 to 6 hours, or until it is firm.

This ice cream will keep in the freezer for a couple of weeks in an airtight container, but it's best when fresh.

HORCHATA

Makes 1 quart (272 g)

....

2½ cups (600 ml) all-natural canned coconut milk

⅓ cup (67 g) organic unrefined cane sugar

¼ cup (60 ml) organic agave

1 tsp pure vanilla extract

½ tsp ground allspice

1 tsp ground cinnamon

1 tbsp (15 ml) dark rum (optional)

Pinch of sea salt

Horchata has historically been made by soaking various nuts and grains and adding spices, extracts, and even alcohol for flavoring. Its variations have been found around the globe for hundreds of years. This ice cream version utilizes the inherent creaminess of coconut milk and builds flavor with pure vanilla, fresh spices, and a hint of rum (which is optional). While tasty on its own, this ice cream pairs wonderfully with coffee, tea, or your favorite root soda.

Use a high-speed or immersion blender to thoroughly mix all of the ingredients. Cover and chill the mixture for at least 1 hour, or overnight.

Add the chilled mixture to your ice cream maker and churn it according to the manufacturer's instructions. Most machines take 10 to 15 minutes depending on the temperature of the mix, and when it's finished it should look like soft serve. Once it's churned, transfer the ice cream to a large freezer-safe container, smooth the top, cover, and freeze it for at least 5 to 6 hours, or until it is firm. If you used rum, it will make the ice cream slightly softer when it is completely set.

Depending on the temperature of your freezer you may want to set the ice cream out for 5 to 10 minutes to soften it before serving. This ice cream will keep in the freezer for a couple of weeks in an airtight container, though it is best when it's fresh.

MANGO HABANERO

This flavor was one of the first we made at FoMu. It had a cult-like following—for good reason. It is bright in taste, vibrant in color, and smooth in texture. Fiery habanero gives it a kick, and cool, sweet mango brings you back for more. The use of fresh, ripe ingredients delivers a show-stopping scoop that everyone needs to try.

Makes 1 quart (272 g)

....

1 cup (240 ml) mango purée (about 2 mangos or 2 cups [330 g] cubed frozen mangos)

2¼ cups (520 ml) all-natural canned coconut milk

1 tbsp (14 g) organic unrefined cane sugar

¼ cup (60 ml) agave

1 habanero pepper, deseeded

Use a high-speed or immersion blender to thoroughly mix the mango purée, coconut milk, sugar, agave, and habanero pepper, paying particular attention that the habanero is completely blended. Cover and chill the mixture in a sealed container for at least 1 hour, or overnight.

Add the chilled mixture to your ice cream maker and churn it according to the manufacturer's instructions. Most machines take 10 to 15 minutes depending on the temperature of the mix, and when it's finished it should look like soft serve. Once it's churned, transfer the ice cream to a wide, shallow, freezer-safe container. Smooth the top, cover, and freeze the finished ice cream for at least 5 to 6 hours, or until it is firm. If the ice cream does not fully set, it will compromise the quality over time. The ice cream will keep for a couple of weeks in an airtight container, but is best enjoyed fresh.

CARDAMOM PISTACHIO

Makes about 1 quart
(272 g)

....

1 cup (150 g) unsalted whole pistachios,
shelled and divided, plus extra for
serving

2⅓ cups (540 ml) all-natural canned
coconut milk

¼ cup (50 g) organic unrefined cane
sugar

¼ cup (60 ml) organic agave

1 tsp ground cardamom

Pinch of sea salt

Kulfi is a traditional Indian-style ice cream that is denser and creamier than conventional American ice cream, inspiring this flavorful combination. It is usually flavored with spices like cardamom and pistachio. Coconut milk provides a rich and creamy foundation for the exotic ingredients as well as a complementary flavor. Grinding the pistachios for the base enriches the flavor, and using whole pistachios for serving adds extra texture and beautiful color.

Place ½ cup (75 g) of the pistachios in a food processor and grind them until they reach the consistency of a chunky paste. Use a high-speed or immersion blender to mix the pistachio paste, coconut milk, sugar, agave, cardamom, and salt. Cover and chill the mixture for at least 2 hours, or overnight.

Once the mixture is chilled, add it to your ice cream maker and churn it according to the manufacturer's instructions. Most machines take 10 to 15 minutes depending on the temperature of the mix, and when it's finished it should look like soft serve. Once it's churned, transfer the ice cream to a wide, freezer-safe container and stir in the remaining whole pistachios, distributing them evenly while making sure to maintain the air churned into the base. Cover the ice cream tightly and freeze it for at least 5 to 6 hours, or until it is firm.

Depending on the temperature of your freezer you may want to set the ice cream out for 5 to 10 minutes to soften it before serving. This ice cream will keep in the freezer for a couple of weeks in an airtight container, but it's best when fresh.

THAI TEA

Makes 1 quart (272 g)

. . . .

Thai tea is commonly found on Southeast Asian restaurant menus, and lately, on trendy café menus. It starts with a strongly brewed Assam or Ceylon black tea, which is mixed with sugar and condensed milk and layered with evaporated or coconut milk. Various spices and extracts may be added for flavor. This recipe is a spin-off of the traditional beverage, with the addition of some deliciously distinctive spices.

2 black or red Thai tea bags or 2 tbsp (4 g) loose leaf tea

½ cup (120 ml) hot water

2 star anise

3 whole cloves

2¼ cups (520 ml) all-natural canned coconut milk

⅓ cup (67 g) unrefined cane sugar

¼ cup (60 ml) agave

Start by making the tea concentrate. Steep 2 times the recommended per serving amount of tea into ½ cup (120 ml) of hot water. Add the star anise and cloves. Let the tea steep for twice the recommended amount of time. Concentrating the tea lessens the added water, improving texture and flavor. Discard the teabag and spices, and let the tea cool to room temperature.

Use a high-speed or immersion blender to thoroughly mix the tea, coconut milk, sugar, and agave. Chill the mixture in a sealed container for at least 1 hour, or overnight.

Add the chilled mixture to your ice cream maker and churn it according to the manufacturer's instructions. Most machines take 10 to 15 minutes depending on the temperature of the mix, and when it's finished it should look like soft serve. Once it's churned, transfer the ice cream to a wide, shallow, freezer-safe container. Smooth the top, cover, and freeze the finished ice cream for at least 5 to 6 hours, or until it is firm.

This ice cream will keep in the freezer for a couple of weeks in an airtight container, but it's best when fresh.

BANOFFEE PIE

Makes about 1 quart (272 g)

. . . .

2 cups (480 ml) all-natural canned coconut milk

2 tbsp (30 ml) organic agave

⅓ cup (67 g) organic unrefined cane sugar

1 cup (225 g) ripe banana, puréed

Pinch of sea salt

½ cup (45 g) all-natural plain graham cracker, roughly chopped

⅓ cup (100 g) dark chocolate, roughly chopped

Vanilla Bean Caramel (page 139) (optional)

I had my first piece of banoffee pie within a month of studying abroad in England. While it's a classic dessert in England, I had never heard of it in the US. It contains simple ingredients, like fresh banana, whipped cream, toffee, and a cookie crust, but it tastes like heaven. Fast forward to FoMu–I had to replicate my beloved Banoffee Pie in ice cream form. This recipe combines fresh banana, dark chocolate, and graham cracker in a creamy coconut base. It is even better served with homemade Vanilla Bean Caramel sauce (page 139). While it may not be traditional, it is certainly delicious.

Use a high-speed or immersion blender to mix the coconut milk, agave, and sugar. Add the puréed banana and salt, and blend until it is completely smooth. Chill the mixture for at least 2 hours, or overnight.

Once the mixture is chilled, add it to your ice cream maker and churn it according to the manufacturer's instructions. Most machines take 10 to 15 minutes depending on the temperature of the mix, and when it's finished it should look like soft serve. Once it's churned, fold in the graham cracker chunks, chocolate, and caramel all at the same time, as to not over mix the ice cream base or caramel. Transfer the ice cream to a large, freezer-safe container, smooth the top, and cover it tightly. Freeze the ice cream for at least 5 to 6 hours, or until it is firm.

This ice cream will keep in the freezer for a couple of weeks in an airtight container, but it's best when fresh.

ROSEWATER SAFFRON

Makes 1 quart (272 g)

....

2½ cups (600 ml) all-natural canned coconut milk

¼ cup (50 g) organic unrefined cane sugar

¼ cup (60 ml) organic agave

1 tsp saffron threads

1 tsp rosewater

Pinch of sea salt

I distinctly remember my grandmother's desserts including a particular flavor when I was a child, but I never knew what it was until I started cooking myself. It was rosewater, which is made by steeping rose petals in water. It is incredibly fragrant and floral, and commonly used in Middle Eastern desserts. Saffron is a vivid and aromatic spice derived from a flower. It has a savory-yet-sweet flavor that is widely used in Mediterranean cuisines. When the two ingredients are paired, they create a unique, fragrant scoop that would impress any ice cream connoisseur—and hopefully my grandmother.

Bring all of the ingredients to a boil in a 2-quart (2-L) heavy saucepan over medium heat, stirring them occasionally, and then remove the pan from heat. Cover the ingredients and let them steep for 30 minutes, then pour the cream mixture through a fine-mesh sieve into a bowl and discard the saffron threads. Cover and chill the mixture for at least 2 hours, or overnight.

Add the chilled mixture to your ice cream maker and churn it according to the manufacturer's instructions. Most machines take 10 to 15 minutes depending on the temperature of the mix, and when it's finished it should look like soft serve. Transfer the churned ice cream to a shallow, freezer-safe container, cover, and freeze it for at least 5 to 6 hours, or until it is firm.

This ice cream will keep in the freezer for a couple of weeks in an airtight container, but it's best when fresh.

TIRAMISU

Makes about 1 quart
(272 g)

. . . .

¼ cup (35 g) espresso beans, finely
ground

2¾ cups (660 ml) all-natural canned
coconut milk

⅓ cup (67 g) organic unrefined cane
sugar

2 tbsp (30 ml) organic agave

Pinch of sea salt

1 tbsp (15 ml) dark rum (optional)

½ tsp pure vanilla extract

½ cup (125 g) Vanilla Shortbread (page
119), room temperature and roughly
chopped

½ cup (125 g) dark chocolate, roughly
chopped

Traditional tiramisu is a dreamy dessert. Creamy, boozy, and a little bitter thanks to coffee and dark chocolate, it is complex-tasting and ethereal in texture. When I was studying abroad, I lived with two women from Italy. One night they casually made a tray of tiramisu and were gracious enough to share it. Even though it was served in a secondhand baking tray with a soup ladle, it was the best tiramisu I've ever had. I ate more than my fair share that day, and since then it has been one of my most favorite desserts. This recipe may not be totally authentic, but it hits all the right notes, all in one scoop.

Bring the ground espresso, coconut milk, sugar, agave, and salt to a simmer in a 2-quart (2-L) heavy saucepan over medium heat, then remove the pan from heat. Cover it and let it steep for 30 minutes, or overnight.

Pour the cream mixture through a fine-mesh sieve into a bowl and discard any espresso grounds. Add the rum, if you're using it, and the vanilla. Cover and chill the mixture for at least 2 hours, or overnight.

Add the chilled mixture to your ice cream maker and churn it according to the manufacturer's instructions. Most machines take 10 to 15 minutes depending on the temperature of the mix, and when it's finished it should look like soft serve, though the rum may cause the ice cream to churn a little softer. Transfer the churned ice cream to a large, shallow, freezer-safe container and fold in the shortbread and dark chocolate, making sure to maintain the air churned into the base. Smooth the top, cover, and freeze it for at least 5 to 6 hours, or until it is firm.

This ice cream will keep in the freezer for a couple of weeks in an airtight container, but it's best when fresh.

BLACK SESAME

Makes 1 quart (272 g)

. . . .

6 tbsp (60 g) black sesame seeds, plus more for serving

2½ cups (600 ml) all-natural canned coconut milk

⅓ cup (67 g) organic unrefined cane sugar

¼ cup (60 ml) organic agave

½ tsp pure vanilla extract

Pinch of sea salt

If you've ever visited Japan or even a Japanese restaurant, you may have noticed Black Sesame ice cream on the menu. It's a common Asian dessert offering reminiscent of a nuttier and slightly more savory peanut butter ice cream. It is unique, eye-catching, and absolutely delicious. Sprinkle some extra black sesame seeds on top for an upscale presentation.

Toast the black sesame seeds in a skillet over medium heat, stirring them occasionally, about 3 to 5 minutes, or until they start to smell nutty. As soon as they are done, remove the pan from the heat and transfer the black sesame seeds to a small food processor. Process the sesame seeds until they are finely ground and start to look like a paste, about 1 minute.

Bring the coconut milk, sugar, agave, vanilla, and salt to a simmer in a 2-quart (2-L) heavy saucepan over medium heat and then add the sesame paste. Remove the pan from heat, cover it, and let it steep for 30 minutes.

Pour the cream mixture through a fine-mesh sieve into a bowl and discard any large seed remnants. Cover and chill the mixture for at least 2 hours, or overnight.

Add the chilled mixture to your ice cream maker and churn it according to the manufacturer's instructions. Most machines take 10 to 15 minutes depending on the temperature of the mix, and when it's finished it should look like soft serve. Transfer the churned ice cream to a large, freezer-safe container, smooth the top, and cover it. Freeze the finished ice cream for at least 5 to 6 hours, or until it is firm.

Serve this ice cream with extra black sesame seeds for a striking treat. It will keep in the freezer for a couple of weeks in an airtight container, but it's best when fresh.

OVER *the* TOP

Who wants cookie dough ice cream without cookie dough? How can you build an epic sundae without hot fudge? What's an ice cream sandwich without a fresh chocolate chip cookie?

These recipes for baked inclusions, toppings, and accompaniments use all of the same principles as my ice cream recipes. They are incredibly delicious and use all-natural, real, plant-based ingredients.

Not only do you feel good eating them, they just taste better. You are able to control the amount and size of the inclusions you want to incorporate into your ice cream, and you can make extra for snacking. All of these recipes are versatile and can be used on their own or as accompaniments to the ice cream recipes. They store well, too, so feel free to double or even triple the batches!

SALTED CHOCOLATE CHIP COOKIES

Makes about 1 dozen

....

2½ cups (300 g) all-purpose flour

½ tsp baking soda

¾ tsp baking powder

½ tsp coarse sea salt

1 cup (250 g) dark chocolate chips or dark chocolate, roughly chopped

2 tbsp (30 ml) melted coconut oil

½ cup (120 ml) all-natural vegan butter

½ cup (100 g) organic light brown sugar

½ cup (100 g) organic cane sugar

¼ cup (60 ml) unsweetened applesauce

1 tsp pure vanilla extract

Flake sea salt (like Gray or Maldon), for sprinkling

Chocolate chip cookies are a staple in almost everyone's recipe library. This recipe is free of dairy and egg, but full of rich, sweet flavor. Real vanilla, a little coconut oil, and the sprinkling of some flake salt take these cookies to the next level of deliciousness. Feel free to try almond extract instead of vanilla for a yummy twist. They are totally addictive on their own, but are over-the-top when sandwiching a scoop of your favorite ice cream flavor. Pro tip—freeze your cookies before making ice cream cookie sammies to prevent breakage. You can even get fancy and roll them in chocolate chips or sprinkles. Freeze chunks of the dough for Chocolate Cookie Dough ice cream (page 49) or late night nibbles!

Preheat your oven to 350°F (177°C). Combine the flour, baking soda, baking powder, and salt in a large bowl. Whisk to combine them, then add the chocolate chips and stir. Set the bowl aside.

Use a stand mixer with a paddle attachment, a hand mixer, or a whisk to combine the coconut oil, butter, brown sugar, and cane sugar. Mix until the mixture is nice and fluffy, then add the applesauce and vanilla. Mix again until the ingredients are well combined. Gradually add the flour mixture until it is just incorporated. Cover the bowl with plastic wrap and chill it for at least 30 minutes, or overnight.

Line a baking sheet or two with parchment paper. Remove the dough from the refrigerator. Using an ice cream scoop, place the dough onto the parchment paper in about ⅓-cup (75-g) scoops, leaving plenty of room for spreading. Sprinkle the dough lightly with flake sea salt.

Bake the cookies for 12 to 14 minutes, or until they are golden on the edges. I tend to underbake cookies and let them set for a few minutes out of the oven to ensure they have a great chew, and to avoid the risk of overbaking. Transfer the cookies to a cooling rack and let them cool until they reach room temperature.

If you're using the cookies for ice cream sammies, place them in the freezer for a stronger composition. These cookies will keep for 1 week at room temperature or for a couple of weeks in the freezer in an airtight container.

CHOCOLATE SANDWICH COOKIE

Every ice cream maker needs a good cookies and cream recipe. But when I first started making ice cream, it was hard to find an all-natural, plant-based chocolate sandwich cookie. Here is my take on everyone's favorite. When you're making this recipe to include in ice cream, save time by making a couple of extra-large cookie sandwiches to chop into large chunks. If you're making the cookies to eat on their own, feel free to use your favorite cookie cutter and cut them to your size preference.

Makes about 24 small cookie sandwiches or more, depending on the cookie cutter

. . . .

Cookies

½ cup (115 g) all-natural vegan butter, at room temperature

½ cup (100 g) organic unrefined cane sugar

3 tbsp (45 ml) organic agave

½ tsp baking soda

¼ tsp kosher salt

¼ tsp pure vanilla extract

1¼ cups (165 g) all-purpose flour

⅓ cup + 1 tbsp (32 g) premium Dutch-process cocoa, plus extra for dusting

Icing

½ cup (115 g) natural vegan butter

¼ cup (55 g) coconut oil

1 tsp vanilla extract

1 tsp kosher salt

2 cups (240 g) organic powdered sugar

To make the cookies, use a handheld mixer or stand mixer fitted with a paddle attachment to combine the butter, sugar, agave, baking soda, salt, and vanilla. Mix on low speed to moisten the mixture, then increase to medium and beat until it is fluffy and light, about 5 minutes. Pause to scrape the bowl and paddle about halfway through.

Sift the flour and cocoa together. With the mixer running on low speed, sprinkle the flour and cocoa mixture into the butter mixture. It might seem dry at first, but continue mixing until it forms a smooth dough. You can use this raw cookie dough immediately or wrap it in plastic and refrigerate it up to 1 week.

Adjust your oven rack to the middle position and preheat the oven to 350°F (177°C). Form the dough into a ball with your hands, then divide it in half and flatten each half into a disk. On a cocoa-dusted surface, roll each disk until it is ¼ inch (6 mm) thick. You can use cookie cutters to cut the dough into shapes, or keep it whole if you're using for ice cream.

Lay the cookie dough on a parchment-lined baking sheet and dock it with a knife to help steam escape. Bake the cookies until they are firm and dry, about 15 to 20 minutes depending on the format. Cool them to room temperature on the baking sheet.

To make the icing, cream the butter and coconut oil with the vanilla and salt in a stand mixer or with a handheld mixer. Slowly add the powdered sugar until the mixture is moist, then increase the mixer speed to medium and beat the mixture until it is creamy and soft, about 5 minutes. Use an offset spatula or pastry bag to top the cookies with the icing. Sandwich the individual or large cookies with the icing.

The cookies will keep for up to 1 week at room temperature or 3 months frozen.

VANILLA SHORT-BREAD

This super simple, classic shortbread recipe is a staple on its own or as an inclusion in many of the ice cream recipes featured in this book. To ensure a clean ingredient list, make sure to buy all-natural, non-hydrogenated vegetable margarine—with none of that funny stuff. Use a good-quality, pure vanilla extract, but feel free to experiment with other extracts for a flavor twist—think almond, lemon, or bergamot. Ice and decorate these cookies for an eye-popping treat. This recipe is versatile, fun, and delicious!

Makes 1 dozen large shortbread cookies

½ lb (230 g) all-natural, non-hydrogenated vegetable margarine

1 cup (200 g) organic unrefined cane sugar

Pinch of sea salt

½ tsp pure vanilla extract

2 cups (240 g) unbleached all-purpose flour

Preheat your oven to 300°F (150°C). Grease a parchment-lined baking sheet tray and set it aside.

With a handheld or stand mixer with paddle attachment, cream together the margarine and sugar until the mixture is light and fluffy. Add the salt and vanilla and mix until they are just combined. Add the flour to the margarine mixture, and mix until it's well combined and no margarine or sugar pockets remain.

Pour the batter onto the baking sheet and press it into the pan, smoothing the surface with your fingers or with a mini rolling pin. Use a fork to prick the dough all over to allow steam to escape and to prevent the shortbread from bubbling as it bakes. Bake the shortbread until it is a light golden brown, about 30 minutes. Remove it from the oven and immediately use a cookie cutter, pizza wheel, or sharp knife to cut it into 12 squares. Do this while the shortbread is still warm; if you wait until it's cool, it won't cut easily. Transfer the shortbread to a rack to cool completely.

You can store the cookies in an airtight container for up to 1 week, or freeze them for up to 1 month.

DOUBLE CHOCOLATE BROWNIES

Makes 1 (9 x 13-inch
[23 x 33-cm]) tray

A good brownie is quite possibly ice cream's most important accessory, and this recipe can certainly hold the title. These brownies are rich and chewy and intensely chocolatey; the optional addition of instant coffee deepens the chocolate flavor while coconut milk adds richness and a subtle but welcome essence. Instead of using eggs to bind the bars, these brownies use fiber-rich and heart-healthy chia seeds to add structure and chew. Dark chocolate chips add texture and extra chocolate flavor, but feel free to substitute your favorite nut or natural candy. Cut these brownies into squares to use them for sundaes or bars, or roughly chop them to use in ice cream or as a topping. They store really well in the freezer, so make extra!

½ cup (42 g) premium Dutch-process cocoa, weighed

4 oz (72 g) unsweetened dark chocolate

1 tsp instant coffee (optional)

¾ tsp sea salt

½ cup (115 g) all-natural vegetable margarine

¼ cup (60 ml) all-natural canned coconut milk

2 tbsp (28 g) ground chia seed

6 tbsp (90 ml) cold water

1 cup (200 g) organic cane sugar

½ cup (100 g) organic dark brown sugar

1 tbsp (15 ml) pure vanilla extract

1½ cups (180 g) all-purpose flour

¼ tsp baking soda

1 cup (250 g) dark chocolate chips or dark chocolate, roughly chopped

Preheat your oven to 350°F (177°C). Grease a 9 x 13–inch (23 x 33–cm) baking pan lined with parchment paper, and set it aside.

Combine the cocoa, unsweetened chocolate, instant coffee, if you're using it, salt, margarine, and coconut milk in a bowl over a pot of simmering water, stirring the ingredients occasionally until the mixture is mostly smooth and melted. While the cocoa mixture melts, add the chia seeds to the cold water and stir until they're well combined. Once the chocolate mixture is melted, add in the sugars and vanilla and stir until they're well. Add the chia mixture to the chocolate mixture and whisk until everything is well combined and smooth.

Combine the flour and baking soda in a small bowl. Add this to the chocolate mixture and stir them together with a spatula until the mixture is just combined.

Transfer the batter to the greased baking pan. Smooth the top and evenly sprinkle it with the dark chocolate.

Bake the brownies for 30 minutes, or until an inserted toothpick comes out clean. Allow the brownies to cool to room temperature in the pan, then chill them in the fridge before slicing them. This will help the brownies slice evenly and cleanly. Store them in an airtight container at room temperature for up to 5 days. Or even better, store them in the freezer for up to 30 days and thaw them one or two at a time to use whenever you please!

CHOCOLATE CAKE

Makes 1 (9-inch
[23-cm]) round cake

· ·

1½ cups (180 g) unbleached all-purpose
flour

1 cup (200 g) organic unrefined cane
sugar

¼ cup (22 g) premium Dutch-process
cocoa

1 tsp baking soda

2 tbsp (30 ml) espresso (optional)

Pinch of sea salt

1 tsp pure vanilla extract

1 tbsp (15 ml) apple cider vinegar

⅓ cup (80 ml) vegetable or neutral-
flavored oil

1 cup (240 ml) cold water

This super simple chocolate cake recipe is versatile and delicious. It is moist and flavorful enough to eat on its own, but it's even better layered with your favorite ice cream or coconut buttercream. Use a high-quality Dutch-process cocoa for a rich flavored cake. Adding a high-quality espresso deepens the chocolate flavor, but is optional. Eat on its own or layer with your favorite ice cream for an amazing ice cream cake!

Preheat your oven to 350°F (177°C). Lightly grease a 9-inch (23-cm) round pan that is at least 2 inches (5 cm) deep.

Whisk together the flour, sugar, cocoa, baking soda, espresso, if you're using it, and salt in a medium-sized bowl. Whisk the vanilla, vinegar, vegetable oil, and water in a separate bowl. Pour the wet ingredients into the bowl of dry ingredients, and stir until they're just combined. Pour the batter into the prepared pan.

Bake the cake for 30 to 35 minutes, or until a toothpick inserted into the center comes out clean.

Store this cake in an airtight container at room temperature for up to 5 days, or freeze it for up to a month.

Note: To make homemade ice cream cake, use a springform pan to layer cake and ice cream. Let set in the freezer for at least 2 hours or overnight. Remove from pan and frost with your favorite buttercream or drizzle with chocolate ganache!

OATMEAL CRUMBLE

This oat crumble recipe is super simple, super clean, and super yummy. It is naturally gluten-, nut-, and soy- free and is a great addition in or on top of almost any ice cream. Add it to yogurt or almond milk for a tasty breakfast. Add chopped nuts, seeds, coconut, or dark chocolate chips for an amazing granola to snack on. It is used in a few ice cream recipes, so feel free to double the batch and freeze for later use.

Makes about 1 quart (272 g)

. . . .

1 cup (200 g) whole rolled oats (certified organic and gluten-free, if desired)

⅔ cup (150 g) oat flour (or oats ground into flour)

Pinch of sea salt

1 tbsp (15 g) ground flax seed

⅓ cup (75 g) light brown sugar

1 tbsp (15 ml) melted coconut oil

¼ cup (60 ml) organic agave

1 tsp pure vanilla extract

Preheat your oven to 350°F (177°C). Grease a parchment-lined baking sheet tray and set it aside. Combine the whole oats, oat flour, salt, flax, and brown sugar in a large bowl. Mix the ingredients with a wooden spoon or spatula until everything is evenly distributed. Add the coconut oil, agave, and vanilla to the bowl and mix until all of the ingredients are well combined.

Pour the crumble onto the baking sheet tray. Bake it for approximately 15 minutes, or until it is golden brown. Stir the crumble while it's baking at 5 and 10 minutes to help break it into smaller chunks.

Allow the crumble to cool completely before storing it in an airtight container. It will keep for 1 week at room temperature, but can be frozen for up to 1 month.

SALTED HONEY-COMB

Makes about 2 cups
(400 g)

....

1¼ cups (250 g) organic unrefined cane
sugar
½ cup (120 ml) organic agave
¼ cup (60 ml) cold water
1 tbsp (13 g) baking soda
Pinch of sea salt

Honeycomb candy, unlike the honeycomb we associate with bees, is essentially an aerated hard caramel. It is a staple in England, but I could only find it in the imported sections of select stores in the US. Fortunately, it is so simple to make at home. It is light and crunchy and reminiscent of burnt caramel in flavor. The magic comes from baking soda, which instantly foams when it is added and creates air pockets as it sets in the sugar. This recipe calls for organic agave instead of corn syrup and a sprinkling of salt to bring out the flavor and balance the sweetness. Feel free to play with other liquid sweeteners like maple syrup or sorghum; both add flavor and are all-natural and vegan friendly. I use honeycomb in ice cream, on ice cream, or as a snack all on its own. Beware: it is addictively good.

Line a baking sheet with greased parchment paper.

Combine the sugar, agave, and water in a medium-sized heavy saucepan over medium-high heat, and stir only until the sugar dissolves. Let the mixture come to a boil and cook it until it reaches around 300°F (150°C) and is a dark amber color—for about 5 minutes.

Turn off the heat and whisk in the baking soda, whisking just enough to get out the lumps. Immediately pour the mixture onto the lined baking sheet, using a heatproof spatula to scrape all of it from the pan—but don't smooth it down or you will lose all of those lovely air pockets. Do not touch it yet! It is so hot and sticky. Immediately sprinkle the surface of the candy with sea salt before it sets. Put the baking sheet in a cool, dry place to cool.

When the candy is hard, break it apart into chunks with your fingers. It is the best when it's fresh, as it absorbs moisture and starts to get chewy very quickly. But rest assured, it can be frozen in a sealed container and enjoyed for a couple of weeks.

TOASTY COCONUT

Makes about 1½ cups
(150 g)

. . . .

2 tbsp (30 ml) maple syrup

½ tsp soy sauce, tamari, or coconut aminos

1 tsp pure vanilla extract

1½ cups (150 g) unsweetened large flake coconut

I love ice cream toppings that come together easily, use simple ingredients, and add an extra level of texture and flavor. Toasting and sweetening natural flake coconut yourself ensures that there are no funny ingredients and that the level of sweetness is to your liking. This recipe uses a little bit of either soy sauce, tamari, or coconut aminos— my favorite—to add depth of flavor and a little bit of salt. It is great on its own, as a topping for ice cream or yogurt, or as a lovely addition to granola or trail mix.

Preheat your oven to 300°F (150°C). Line a sheet pan with parchment paper, and set it aside.

Whisk the maple syrup, soy sauce, and vanilla together in a bowl until they're completely smooth. Add the flake coconut and mix until it is evenly coated in the mixture. Spread the mixture out onto the parchment-lined sheet pan and bake it, stirring it every 5 minutes until it's evenly browned and crispy, about 10 minutes. Watch the sheet closely, as coconut can over-brown quickly.

Store your toasty coconut in a sealed container in a cool, dry place for up to 1 week.

CHAI-CANDIED PECANS

Makes about 1 quart
(272 g)

• •

½ cup (100 g) organic unrefined cane
sugar

2 tsp (5 g) ground cinnamon

1 tsp ground ginger

½ tsp ground cardamom

½ tsp ground allspice

¼ tsp ground cloves

¼ tsp ground black pepper

4 cups (400 g) pecans, roughly chopped

¼ cup (60 ml) melted coconut oil

¼ cup (60 ml) pure maple syrup

Pinch of salt

Candying nuts can seem daunting, but this recipe is a foolproof way to make pecans dazzle. It uses traditional chai tea spices for a twist on your standard candied nut. Feel free to omit the spices if you are out or not a fan, but the full combination of flavors really makes these pecans special. Use them as a topping, for snacking, or on your favorite oatmeal.

Preheat your oven to 350°F (177°C). Line a sheet pan with parchment paper and set it aside.

Mix the sugar, cinnamon, ginger, cardamom, allspice, cloves, and black pepper together in a small bowl, and set it aside.

Combine the pecans, coconut oil, maple syrup, and salt, stirring to evenly coat the pecans. Add the sugar and spice mixture to the pecans and stir until everything is well combined and the pecans are evenly coated. Transfer the pecans to the sheet pan and bake them for 10 minutes, stirring them halfway through. Remove them from the oven and let them cool on the baking sheet. Once they're completely cool, transfer them to an airtight container and store them in the refrigerator for up to 1 month.

Note: While delicious on almost any flavor, Chai Pecans are perfect to embellish my Caramel Pecan Pie ice cream (page 45)!

CANDIED CACAO

Makes about 1½ cups
(250 g)

· ·

½ cup (100 g) sugar
2 tbsp (30 ml) water
1 tbsp (15 ml) agave
1 cup (100 g) cacao nibs
1 tbsp (15 ml) melted coconut oil

Cacao nibs are dried, fermented, and roasted cacao beans. They are the pure and healthy cousin of the chocolate that you know and love. They are crunchy, bitter, and intensely chocolate-tasting, but they are not naturally sweet. In this recipe, cacao nibs are mixed with caramelized sugar to produce a crunchy, savory-sweet treat. Break it into pieces and eat it on its own, or use it to top your favorite flavor. It's a unique and healthy complement to your favorite scoop.

Line a baking sheet with parchment, spray it with a nonstick cooking spray, and set it aside.

Combine the sugar, water, and agave in a small saucepan. Stir the mixture well until the sugar is moistened, then place the pan over medium heat and continue to stir for a couple of minutes as the sugar dissolves. Brush down the sides of the pan with a wet pastry brush to remove any stray sugar crystals.

Insert a candy thermometer. Cook the syrup without stirring it until it is a medium amber color, around 330°F (165°C). It will take around 5 minutes but keep a close eye! Remove the pan from the heat and stir in the cacao nibs. Once they're coated with the caramel, add the coconut oil and stir it in well. The oil will help the cacao nibs separate a little bit and will make the mixture easier to spread.

Scrape the candy out onto the prepared baking sheet and spread it into a thin, even layer. Allow it to cool and harden completely at room temperature.

Break the candy into small pieces to eat on its own or use it to top your favorite ice cream. The sharp chocolate flavor pairs well with Chocolate Pudding (page 14), Natural Peanut Butter (page 17) and Salted Caramel (page 21). Store it in an airtight container in a cool, dry place for up to 2 weeks.

SPICED PEPITAS

"Pepitas" is a fancy name for pumpkin seeds without the shell. They are a beautiful green color, really tasty, and good for you. This recipe is a unique twist on your plain old candied nut. It is salty, sweet, spicy, and super versatile. I love it on Vanilla Bean ice cream (page 13) or on its own as a snack.

Makes about 2 cups
(200 g)

· ·

2 cups (200 g) pepitas

1 tbsp (15 ml) melted coconut oil

⅓ cup (67 g) organic unrefined cane sugar

1 tsp chili powder

1 tsp ground cinnamon

½ tsp salt

½ tsp cayenne pepper

Preheat your oven to 350°F (177°C). Line a baking sheet with parchment, spray it with nonstick spray, and set it aside.

Mix the pepitas, coconut oil, sugar, chili powder, cinnamon, salt, and cayenne pepper in a medium bowl until the pepitas are well coated. Spread the pepitas in a single layer on the baking sheet. Bake until they are fragrant and golden, stirring them occasionally—it should take about 15 minutes, but keep a close watch because nuts and seeds can burn easily.

Remove the pepitas from the oven and separate them with a fork while they are still warm. Let them cool completely on the pan before storing them in an airtight container for up to a week in a cool, dry place.

DARK CHOCOLATE FUDGE

Makes about 1½ cups (360 ml)

. . . .

4 oz (113 g) unsweetened chocolate

½ cup (120 ml) all-natural canned coconut milk

½ cup (100 g) organic unrefined cane sugar

¼ cup (60 ml) organic agave

¼ tsp sea salt

½ tsp pure vanilla extract

This is no thin chocolate syrup recipe. This is a rich, flavorful, decadent fudge that will replace any fudge recipe you have used in the past, vegan or not. Unheated, it is almost the texture of fudge candy. Heated, it is a thick, pourable, glistening adornment for your favorite scoop. It comes together in a pinch, and keeps for a long time in the fridge, so there is really no good reason not to have it on hand all the time!

Place the unsweetened chocolate in a metal bowl.

Combine the coconut milk, sugar, agave, and salt in a small saucepan. Cook the mixture over medium-high heat, stirring it frequently with a heatproof spatula, until the sugar is completely dissolved and the mixture is approximately 150°F (65°C), about 7 minutes.

Pour the warm coconut milk mixture over the unsweetened chocolate and let it sit for 30 seconds to 1 minute.

Stir the chocolate with a spatula until the mixture is smooth and the chocolate is completely melted. Continue to blend it with a whisk until the ingredients are fully combined and smooth. It should look glossy and thick and hold slightly to the whisk when removed.

Add the vanilla and transfer the mixture to a storage container. Allow it to cool completely before covering it with a lid. Store it sealed in the fridge for a couple of weeks.

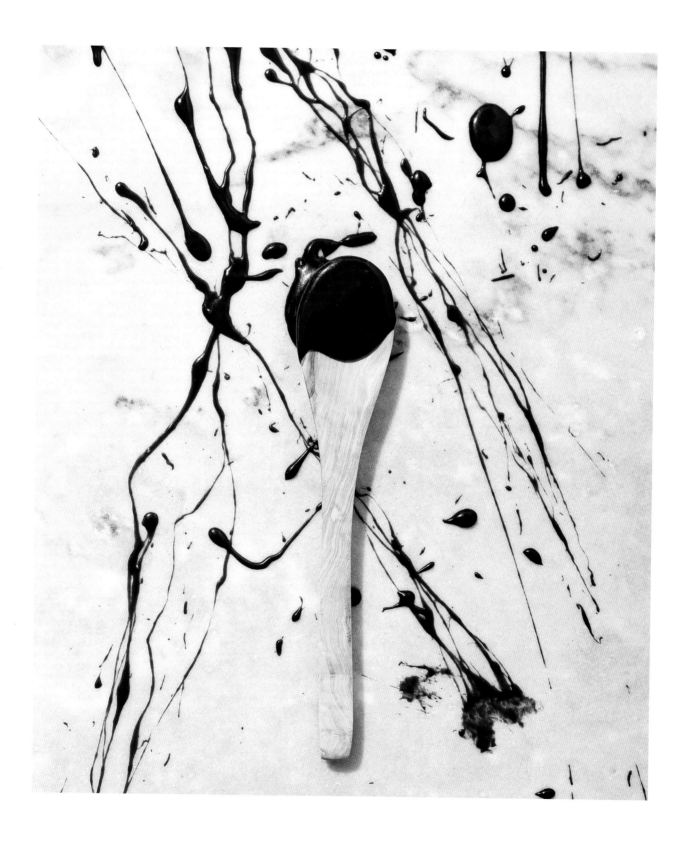

VANILLA BEAN CARAMEL

Makes about 1 quart
(1 L)

. . . .

3 cups (600 g) organic unrefined cane sugar

¾ cup (180 ml) water

¼ tsp lemon juice

1 tbsp (15 ml) agave

2½ cups (600 ml) coconut milk

1 tbsp (15 ml) vanilla extract

½ tsp vanilla bean seeds, about 3 beans, with seeds scraped out

¼ tsp sea salt

If you are anything like me, you could eat caramel by the spoonful. It is one of my favorite additions to almost any ice cream, but also to café drinks and baked goodies, too. Unlike other caramel recipes, this recipe is relatively foolproof but still out-of-this-world delicious. You would never believe it is dairy-free! The real vanilla bean flecks deepen the flavor and elevate the presentation.

Combine the sugar, water, lemon juice, and agave in a large saucepan over medium heat. Cook, occasionally brushing the sides of the pan with a pastry brush dipped in cool water to remove any sugar crystals that may collect, until the sugar is a deep caramel color, smells toasty, and registers 325°F (163°C) on a candy thermometer, about 10 minutes. Remove the sugar from heat and stir in the coconut milk, then return the caramel over the heat and bring it back to a boil. Once it comes to a boil, cook for an additional 5 minutes, until the caramel registers between 215 to 220°F (420 to 430°C) on a candy thermometer. Remove the caramel from heat and allow it to cool for about 30 minutes.

Stir in the vanilla extract, vanilla bean seeds, and salt. Once the caramel is completely cool, store it in an airtight container in the fridge for up to 1 week or in the freezer for 1 month.

WHIPPED COCONUT CREAM

Coconut cream is a magical ingredient. Naturally sweet, floral, and creamy, it needs very little help to shine. This simple and easy recipe showcases the wonderful flavor and texture of coconut cream and is versatile enough to use for any dessert or beverage. Use pure vanilla extract for a traditional sundae topping, or feel free to play around with extracts for a unique twist.

Makes about 1 quart
(1 L)

....

1½ cups (360 ml) all-natural canned coconut cream or coconut milk
½ tsp pure vanilla extract
½ cup (46 g) organic powdered sugar

Chill your coconut cream in the refrigerator for at least 2 hours or overnight to allow the fat to rise to the top and separate. Chill a large mixing bowl before whipping.

After the coconut cream has chilled, pour out any excess liquid and reserve the thicker cream for whipping. Place the thick cream in your chilled mixing bowl and beat it with a handheld or stand mixer until it is creamy, 30 seconds to 1 minute. Then add the vanilla and powdered sugar and mix until everything is creamy and smooth—about another minute. If the mixture is not whipping to peaks, try re-chilling the bowl.

Transfer the whipped coconut cream to an airtight container and use it immediately or refrigerate it for up to 1 week.

ACKNOWLEDGMENTS

I cannot help but use this book as a podium to thank all of the folks that have helped bring it to fruition and also to acknowledge those who have influenced me along the way. No words can possibly articulate my gratitude, but I hope that these pages serve as a forever reminder.

Starting from day one, I have to credit my parents, Sam and Alice Jalal, for taking me to the farm and packing what I thought were the grossest school lunches. Those humble and diverse experiences built my character and influenced the way I eat, work, and nourish my family today.

I'd like to thank my family and friends for never uttering a word of doubt, being endlessly supportive, and always being there during crazy, unpredictable days.

I'd like to thank Bobby Rook and Marc Cooper for providing opportunity and insight. Our story wasn't built without some mentorship and good fortune.

I'd like to thank Matthew Moynihan, Erin Ross, Ryan Hardiman, and Kathrine Davidson for being part of our founding FoMu crew and for helping to ideate what would become some pretty phenomenal flavors.

I'd like to thank Matthew Woellert and Megan Calipari for testing and growing our recipe repertoire and for providing support through the writing and photography process.

I'd like to thank Jason and Emily Kan, Catrine Kelty, and Michelle Barrett Ceramics for making my ice cream look so beautiful and for having so much fun in the process.

I'd like to thank Page Street Publishing for so kindly offering me the opportunity to document years of hard work. It is something that I had always wanted to do, but could never muster up the confidence to initiate myself.

I'd like to thank my boys—Kellan, Asher, and Grayson—for being so vibrant, adaptable, and loving. They inspire me to do better, look further, and never give up. They have influenced my food philosophy, recipes, and ongoing integrity. I hope this book inspires them to always persistently pursue their passions.

And finally, I'd like to thank my husband, Hin. Without his encouragement, hard work, and partnership, FoMu and this book would never be. He always has my back, catches me mid-fall, and makes sure everything is ok. He is the best dad, coworker, and friend I could ever ask for. To think, this all started with our (almost) daily ice cream dates.

ABOUT *the* AUTHOR

Deena Jalal is the owner and founder of FoMu Ice Cream. She has been reinventing recipes and brand building since 2010. In the process she developed a profound respect for food, sustainability, and everything local. She's a proud mom of three little boys, smitten wife of FoMu's co-founder, and clinically diagnosed sunshine addict. When she's not at FoMu, you can find her at the farm, on a trail, or in the kitchen. Find out more about FoMu at www.fomuicecream.com or visit one of her many shops in Boston, Massachusetts.

INDEX